A Map of Selves

A Map of Selves defines a concept of selfhood, radically different from the Cartesian, neo-Humean, materialist and animalist concepts which now dominate analytical philosophy of mind. A self, as this book defines it, is an enduring substance with a quality which is its constant possession, which it does not share with any other substance, and which is often remembered by it as its own. The author maintains that *we* are selves as so defined. He criticises the panpsychist theory that material objects are composed of selves analogous to ours, and argues, further, for the existence of at least one transcendent self, whose activity explains both our own existence and the existence of the natural world. He ends by considering whether things would be worse for us if selves as the book defines them did not exist, and we were, as some philosophers suppose we are, just brains, or sequences of mental events, or hylemorphic structures, or subjects which last no longer than the specious present.

Nathan's carefully argued and original book will be of interest to researchers in metaphysics and philosophical psychology, and to their students.

N.M.L. Nathan is a former Reader in Philosophy and now Hon. Senior Fellow in the University of Liverpool, UK. His books include *Evidence and Assurance* (1980), *Will and World* (1992), and *The Price of Doubt* (Routledge, 2000).

Routledge Studies in Metaphysics

Authority and the Metaphysics of Political Communities
Gabriele De Anna

Language and Word
A Defence of Linguistic Idealism
Richard Gaskin

Neo-Aristotelian Perspectives on Formal Causation
Edited by Ludger Jansen and Petter Sandstad

A Powerful Particulars View of Causation
R. D. Ingthorsson

Neo-Aristotelian Metaphysics and the Theology of Nature
Edited by William M. R. Simpson, Robert C. Koons, and James Orr

Death, Determinism, and Meaning
Stephen Maitzen

A Case for Necessitarianism
Amy Karofsky

E.J. Lowe and Ontology
Edited by Miroslaw Szatkowski

A Map of Selves
Beyond Philosophy of Mind
N. M. L. Nathan

For more information about this series, please visit: https://www.routledge.com/Routledge-Studies-in-Metaphysics/book-series/RSM

A Map of Selves
Beyond Philosophy of Mind

N.M.L. Nathan

LONDON AND NEW YORK

First published 2022
by Routledge
4 Park Square, Milton Park, Abingdon, Oxon OX14 4RN

and by Routledge
605 Third Avenue, New York, NY 10158

Routledge is an imprint of the Taylor & Francis Group, an informa business

© 2022 N.M.L. Nathan

The right of N.M.L. Nathan to be identified as author of this work has been asserted by them in accordance with sections 77 and 78 of the Copyright, Designs and Patents Act 1988.

All rights reserved. No part of this book may be reprinted or reproduced or utilised in any form or by any electronic, mechanical, or other means, now known or hereafter invented, including photocopying and recording, or in any information storage or retrieval system, without permission in writing from the publishers.

Trademark notice: Product or corporate names may be trademarks or registered trademarks, and are used only for identification and explanation without intent to infringe.

British Library Cataloguing-in-Publication Data
A catalogue record for this book is available from the British Library

Library of Congress Cataloging-in-Publication Data
Names: Nathan, N. M. L., author.
Title: A map of selves : beyond philosophy of mind / N.M.L. Nathan.
Description: Abingdon, Oxon ; New York, NY : Routledge, 2022. | Series: Routledge studies in metaphysics | Includes bibliographical references and index.
Identifiers: LCCN 2021055776 (print) | LCCN 2021055777 (ebook) | ISBN 9781032228501 (hbk) | ISBN 9781032228518 (pbk) | ISBN 9781003274483 (ebk)
Subjects: LCSH: Self (Philosophy)
Classification: LCC BD438.5 .N28 2022 (print) | LCC BD438.5 (ebook) | DDC 126--dc23/eng/20220118
LC record available at https://lccn.loc.gov/2021055776
LC ebook record available at https://lccn.loc.gov/2021055777

ISBN: 978-1-032-22850-1 (hbk)
ISBN: 978-1-032-22851-8 (pbk)
ISBN: 978-1-003-27448-3 (ebk)

DOI: 10.4324/9781003274483

Typeset in Sabon
by KnowledgeWorks Global Ltd.

Sheer off, disseveral, a star.

To Alix

Contents

Acknowledgements   ix

Introduction   1

1   Human Selves   3

    1.1   *A Remembered Quality*   3
    1.2   *Introspection?*   6
    1.3   *Unconsciousness*   7
    1.4   *Volition*   8
    1.5   *Disseveralities*   10
    1.6   *Substances*   17
    1.7   *Embodied*   21
    1.8   *Free*   30
    1.9   *Ulterior?*   40

2   Ulterior Selves?   45

    2.1   *Continuity*   46
    2.2   *Ignorance and Simplicity*   48
    2.3   *The Confinement of Qualities*   49

3   At Least One Transcendent Self   56

    3.1   *Exclusion*   56
    3.2   *Evidential Sufficient Reason*   59
    3.3   *An Explanatory Inference*   62
    3.4   *The Causation of Disseveralities*   64
    3.5   *Essence and Existence*   69
    3.6   *An Argument from Causation*   69
    3.7   *An Argument from Existence*   73

4 If Selves did not Exist 80

Excursus 87
    A: *Primitive Modality* 87
    B: *Consensual Propositions* 91

References 96
Index 100

Acknowledgements

I am grateful to Paul Helm and William Charlton for reading and criticising an earlier version of this book. My thanks for their suggestions to Routledge's two anonymous referees, and my thanks to Barry Dainton, Sebastian Gardner and Paul Snowdon for their encouragement.

INTRODUCTION

In this book, I define a concept of selfhood and maintain that selves, as so defined, exist. The concept I define is Cartesian to the extent that it requires a self to be a substance which endures for longer than an episode of experience, but not to the extent that it requires a self to be essentially or whenever it exists conscious. It has been complained that 'there is something curiously formal and empty' about the Cartesian concept of a thinking substance.[1] What, as distinct from its thinking, is that which thinks? Descartes does not say. For him, it is an '*I know not what*'.[2] How then, by contrast, do I define a self? As an enduring substance with a *quality*, which is its constant possession, which it does not share with any other substance, and which, when not remembered by it as its own, still has an affinity with a quality which someone remembers having had.

In the first chapter of the book I maintain that, with selfhood taken as I define it, *we* are selves. Chapter 2 is about the quasi-Leibnizian or panpsychist theory that material objects are composed of selves analogous to ours. Such entities I call ulterior selves, and I criticise what are I think the most plausible arguments for their existence. Chapter 3 is about transcendent selves, by which I mean ones that cause both the existence of any non-abstract nonselves there may be which are not composed of selves, and the existence of all those selves which do not cause the existence of every other self. I argue for the existence of at least one transcendent self. Chapter 4 is about how life might have been for us if we had been, what some philosophers believe we really are, not selves but brains, or what brains constitute, or hylemorphic structures, or causally or mnemonically united sequences of mental occurrences, or systems of capacities for conscious stream-like experiences, or conscious subjects which last no longer than the specious present.

A further word on Chapters 1 to 3.

Chapter 1 affirms the existence of human selves, at least sometimes embodied, at least sometimes free, and each one endowed, throughout its existence, with a quality not possessed by any other self. What quality? Suppose you see a scarlet poppy, and, afterwards, remember what saw the poppy as well as what was seen. Then you may remember a quality which what saw it had, a quality too familiar to you to be often noticed. Since you were what saw the poppy, this quality was yours. You may believe, with no chance of being confuted, that the quality was yours before you saw the poppy, and, what is more, that it continues to be yours for as long as you exist. You may then believe, with reason, that it is uniquely yours. You see a scarlet poppy, and then remember what saw it. That was my example. I could as well have taken a case not of seeing but of deciding. You decide, say, to drink more brandy, and then remember not just what was decided but also the decider. Remembering the decider, you remember a quality. This quality was uniquely yours and will continue to be yours alone.

In Chapter 2, I criticise arguments for the existence of ulterior selves, for the doctrine that there are material objects composed of selves analogous to ours. Material objects in this doctrine are defined not as three-dimensional solids filled with coloured stuff of some sort, but rather as substantial nonselves of a certain kind, events in which cause experiences as of such solids. If they are substantial nonselves, material objects may still be composed of selves, and such selves may be analogous to ours. My criticisms emerge from an *Auseinandersetzung* with some current panpsychist writings and with certain parts of McTaggart's *Nature of Existence*.

In Chapter 3, I maintain that at least one transcendent self exists. I say nothing about how many such selves there are, or about how many, if any, are embodied. Could it be that the only transcendent self is the one forever active and never embodied God of Judaism or Islam? Or that the only transcendent selves are the Persons of the Christian Trinity, and that the one and only embodied transcendent self is the Word, the second Person, who became incarnate as a man? These questions I do not discuss. For the truth of an ostensibly revealed religion there is, conceivably, some sound argument. From its conclusion the answers to these questions might fall out. But I offer no such argument. Why, though, should we believe that there is even one transcendent self? I propose an explanatory inference. To be explained is the existence of non-abstract particulars which are not transcendent selves; to explain this we can postulate at least one transcendent self. The inference employs a restricted principle of sufficient reason, together with the principle that an explanation of the non-emptiness of a class of things must postulate the existence of at least one non-member of the class. It is not an inference from the existence of contingent beings to the existence of at least one necessary being.

Notes

1 Armstrong (1968), 23
2 '*Istud nescio quid mei*' (*Second Meditation*, 20. Rendered as 'this puzzling "I"' in the Cottingham, Murdoch and Stoothoff translation.)

1 HUMAN SELVES

Selves, as I define them, are enduring substances of which this is true: for each, there is a quality which is its constant possession, which is never shared with any other substance, and which, if not remembered as its own, still has an affinity with a quality that someone remembers having had. Do selves, as thus defined, exist? Well, *we* exist, and first I maintain that we are selves as thus defined. Our embodiment and our freedom I turn to after that.

1.1 A Remembered Quality

If you are a self as I define a self, you have a constantly possessed quality. By a quality, I mean a non-relational property, an instance of which can be experienced, imagined or remembered. A property is relational if that a particular has it entails that some other particular exists. My overcoat has the relational property of being shabbier than yours. When you are conscious, you have a relational property. When you are conscious, your consciousness is about something: it has an intentional object. This intentional object may or may not exist. If you wish you were in London, the intentional object of your consciousness does exist. If you are thinking about Neptune or a unicorn, it does not. But whether or not your consciousness has an existent intentional object, there will be a way in which that object is presented to you: your consciousness will have an intentional content.[1] And, as I assume, this intentional content is a particular, distinct from you but dependent on you for its existence. Scarlet is a paradigm quality. You may object that for something to be scarlet is for it to look scarlet under normal conditions, and that nothing can look to be some way unless there is someone other than it to whom it looks that way, which makes scarlet relational. But then what is meant by 'x looks scarlet under normal conditions'? 'That under normal conditions x looks to be what looks scarlet under normal conditions'? A regress beckons which can only be halted if 'scarlet' is at some point given a non-relational sense.

Suppose you see a scarlet poppy and afterwards remember seeing it. Then you remember not just what was seen, but, as well, what saw it. And

DOI: 10.4324/9781003274483-2

if you remember what saw it, then what saw it can only have been you. But if you remember not just what was seen but what saw what was seen, then you will cognise a property F of what saw what was seen, a property other than the property of seeing the poppy. Is this property F a quality? It, or an instance of it, is remembered. So, if it is non-relational, then it is a quality. And it is non-relational. That you saw the poppy entails that the poppy existed as well as you. That you had the property F does not entail that any particular existed besides you. Or suppose, if you like, that you have a visual experience *as of* a scarlet poppy, and then afterwards remember not just the content of this experience but, as well, that by which the experience was enjoyed.[2] If it is a case of memory, then it was by you that the experience was enjoyed. However, if you remember not just the content of the visual experience but what had the visual experience, then you will remember a property F of what had the visual experience, a property other than the property of having the visual experience. Is this other property a quality? Yes, if it is non-relational. And it is non-relational. That you had the visual experience entails that the content of the experience existed as well as you. And the content of the experience is a particular distinct from you. But that you had F does not entail that any particular existed as well as you. Did you have F before you saw the scarlet poppy or had the visual experience as of a scarlet poppy? Do you have F still? You may well think that F has been yours for as long as you have existed and will be yours for as long as you continue to exist. I can find no cogent argument which shows that you would be mistaken.

Nobody denies that each one of us can say, of every experience enjoyed by that one of us, 'whatever it is like for me to have the experience, it is *for me* that it is like that to have it'.[3] But some writers go further. 'What-it-is like-ness is properly speaking what-it-is like-*for-me*-ness'. And the for-me-ness of experience does not 'consist simply in the experience *occurring* in someone (a me)'. Rather, it is a bona fide *phenomenal* dimension of consciousness'.[4] Thus Zahavi and Kriegel. And according to Zahavi, 'one does not grasp for-me-ness by inspecting a self-standing quale, in the same way that one grasps the taste of lemon or the smell of mint...the "me" of for-me-ness is not in the first instance an aspect of *what* is experienced but of how it is experienced; not an object of experience but a constitutive manner of experiencing'. Does he mean that when you remember what had a visual experience as of a scarlet poppy, there is no quality of what had the experience that you remember but only a for-me-ness manner in which the experience was enjoyed? If so, I disagree. Zahavi holds that this ubiquitous dimension of first-personal self-givenness is to be identified with 'the experiential core self', and that this identification gives us 'a kind of middle position' between the two opposing views ...that the self is some kind of unchanging soul-substance ...distinct from and ontologically independent of the mental experiences ...it is the subject of, and that the self is 'a bundle of experiences'.[5] I cannot see that even if there is this ubiquitous dimension of experience, our recognition of it would provide us with an alternative to these two opposing views. We still have the question: What owns or is the subject of an experience with for-me-ness? Is this experience owned by what has a quality, or is it owned just by a bundle of experiences of which the experience is a member?

How do you know that what saw the poppy had a quality unless you know that you remember seeing the poppy and that you do not just seem to remember seeing it? How do you know that you remember seeing the poppy, and do not just seem to remember this? And even if you do somehow know that what saw the poppy had a quality, how do you know that this is a quality that you yourself now have, or had before you saw the poppy, let alone a quality that you have whenever you exist? I reply that I do not aim to show that we *know* that we each have a constantly possessed quality. I aim rather to *explain* the doctrine that we do, and then, having explained it, and affirmed it, to rebut the one plausible argument that I can find which concludes that it is false. It would be beside the point to object that I am assuming the workability of a perceptual model of introspective knowledge or assuming that knowledge of our constant qualities is obtainable by 'inner sense'. Knowledge is not my topic.

How would things stand with us if it were false that we each have a constantly possessed quality? Would the falsity of that doctrine exclude your moral responsibility for past actions, or prevent you from planning for the future? Would the falsity of the doctrine license that belief in our merely fleeting existence which in the East is sometimes seen as a precondition of our final escape from all suffering? Such questions are deferred until Chapter 4.

Nobody will allege the falsity of the doctrine that we each have a constantly possessed quality just on the grounds that we do not know that it is true. Are there more plausible arguments for the doctrine's falsity? I can find just one. '...When I enter most intimately into what I call *myself*, I always stumble on some particular perception or other, of heat or cold, light or shade, love or hatred, pain or pleasure. I never can catch *myself* at any time without a perception, and never can observe anything but the perception'.[6] Presumably, Hume also thought that when he entered most intimately into what he called himself, he never caught any quality but that of which he had a perception, and never caught a quality of what had the perception. Someone might say this: if there really were a quality of what had the perception, then Hume would have caught it; he did not catch it; so, there is no such quality.

An objection to this argument is that although some people say that they have the same negative experience as Hume, others have, or say they have, a different, more positive experience. In an often-quoted passage, Gerard Manley Hopkins wrote of 'my consciousness and feeling of myself, that taste of myself, of *I* and *me* above and in all things, which is more distinctive than the taste of ale or alum, more distinctive than the smell of walnut leaf or camphor…'.[7] If you say that Hume's negative experience can be explained only if there is no quality to be caught, then why can I not say that only if there *is* a quality to be caught can the seeming experience of Hopkins be explained? The answer, I am afraid, is that there are ways to explain both kinds of experiences without assuming that either is veridical. We might say that Hume thought he did not catch the quality not because it was not there but because it was too familiar for him to notice. He would have noticed it had some striking contrast been available between it and some different quality of the same general kind, as between the scarlet of a poppy and the yellow of its surrounding wheat. But in the case of your own constant quality, there is no such presented contrast. Even if other selves have constant qualities different from the quality of yours, neither Hume nor anyone else is aware of the quality of any self other than his own. If you were never aware of more than one colour, then that colour would be too familiar for you to notice. What about the experience that Hopkins thought he had? Someone might say that he thought he caught the quality not because it was there but because he wanted it to be, and that he wanted it to be there because he thought that only if we each have different constant qualities can we be many. I affirm then, without claiming to know as much, that we each have a constantly possessed quality revealed by memory.

1.2 Introspection?

Can your constantly possessed quality be revealed not only by memory but also by introspection: can it be revealed by an awareness simultaneous with what that awareness reveals? Sometimes, when I have a visual experience as of, say, a scarlet poppy, I seem also to have an experience as of an inner something now having that visual experience. Is this experience as of an inner something veridical? Is it an experience *of* an inner something? It is not quite easy to see how what has the experience can be identical to what the experience is as of. As we are reminded by proponents of the 'systematic elusiveness of the self', a knife cannot cut itself, nor a fingertip touch itself. But things can be made clearer if time references are introduced. At time t1, I have a visual experience of a scarlet poppy. At time t, I have an experience of an inner something having an experience of a scarlet poppy. I am the subject of the time t experience, and I was the subject of the time t1 experience. The inner something of which, at time t, I have an experience, is me as I was at time t1. My time t1 experience of a scarlet poppy is seamlessly followed, without any interval of unconsciousness, by my time t experience of an inner something having an experience as of a scarlet poppy.[8] It is true that if at a certain time you have a visual experience as of a scarlet poppy, then you cannot at that same time also be aware of now having that visual experience, and so be aware of yourself as you now are. To avoid the dubious postulation of a single subject of two different simultaneous experiences, we might postulate a single experience with a complex intentional content. One part of the content will represent a scarlet poppy, another part will represent your experience as of the poppy. But since at a certain time you have an experience of the poppy, you cannot at that same time have a *complete* awareness of yourself as you then are without having an awareness of your experience as of the poppy. Suppose that you do then have a complete awareness of yourself as you then are. Then you must have an awareness of your experience as of the poppy. And cannot have a complete awareness of yourself as you then are without also having an awareness of your awareness of your experience as of the poppy. And so on ad infinitum. It looks then as if you cannot have a complete awareness of yourself as you then are without having an experience with an infinitely complex content. But so far as I can see, this does not mean that you cannot be aware at t of a quality that you have at t.

1.3 Unconsciousness

Striving to sustain in the face of our ostensible intervals of unconsciousness the Cartesian thought that we are essentially and always conscious, one philosopher has speculated that we '…exist in a time order different from that in which [we] are deemed to have periods of unconsciousness', and that, though undergoing periods of seeming unconsciousness by virtue of intermittently participating in physical time, we are, in our own time order, always conscious.[9] But suppose that if, as I maintain, the quality revealed by memory is one that you possess whenever you exist. Then by having this quality, you can continue to exist not only in a period in which you are deemed to be unconscious but also in a period in which you really are unconscious. It is not necessary to speculate that you exist in a time order different from the one in which you are deemed to be unconscious. It is not necessary to embrace either the Cartesian doctrine that you are somehow always conscious, or the Humean doctrine that 'when my perceptions are removed for any time, as by sound sleep; so long am I insensible of myself; and may be truly said not to exist'.[10] It is equally unnecessary to suppose that all entities akin to you are even *sometimes* conscious. An entity may exist and then finally cease to exist without ever having been conscious. Since one cannot remember anything without being conscious, this forever unconscious entity cannot itself have remembered having had any quality. But for as long as it existed, this entity may have had a quality with an affinity to a quality which someone remembers having had. And for an entity to be a self, as I defined selfhood, it is necessary not for it to have a quality which *it* remembers having had, but rather for it to have a quality with an affinity to one that *someone* remembers having had. A forever unconscious entity can then be a self. Nor, for an entity to be a self, is it even necessary for it to have a *capacity* to be conscious.

1.4 Volition

You see a scarlet poppy and then afterwards remember the quality of what saw it. This quality, I affirm, is always yours. When I used this example in the Introduction, I said that I could as well have taken a case not of seeing but of deciding: having decided, say, to drink more brandy you remember the decider as well as what was decided, and remembering the decider, you remember a quality, a quality that is always yours. I think, however, that in the case of deciding, you may remember not only a quality which is always yours but also something perhaps best described as an *intensification* of a quality which is always yours. A comparable occurrence would be an increase in the brightness or saturation of a constant hue. Deciding is a species of willing. Other species of willing include trying or making an effort, attending, judging or mentally assenting and forming an intention. Common to these different species of willing is a certain quality. When one has an experience as of something, the experiencing is as it were transparent: what has the experience has a quality, and the experience may be as of something with a quality, but no further quality can be attributed to the experiencing itself. Thinking is at least sometimes thus transparent too. But not willing. What wills has a quality that we may remember having. Willing may require what wills to envisage something which, were it actual, would have a quality. But willing has a quality of its own. This quality, common to deciding, attending, mentally assenting, and the rest, we can call volitional.[11] And the instances of this volitional quality can be described as intensifications of the quality which is always yours. This makes willing not an event caused by the agent but rather an event *in* the agent. If the agent is a substance and there are events which the agent causes, then the difficulty arises on which Broad put his finger when he asked 'How can an event possibly be determined to happen at a certain date if its total cause contained no factor to which the notion of date has any application? And how can the notion of date have any application to anything which is not an event?'[12] But if volitions are events in the agent rather than events caused by the agent, then it is perfectly consistent to say that though the agent is indeed a substance, and substances are not causes, still volitions are events which may themselves be causes and in which the agent, as participant, is intimately involved. We are inclined to think that there is an intimacy between selves and their volitions which is absent from the relation between selves and the thoughts which strike them or between selves and the experiences which they undergo. An especially intimate relation between selves and their volitions seems required by the fact that it is for what they will that selves are praised or blamed, as they are not praised or blamed for the thoughts that strike them or for the experiences that they undergo. This special intimacy is allowed for if the volition of a self is an event which takes place in a self rather than an event which the self causes. I am not insisting that it is *only* by regarding agents as substantial selves with constant qualities whose intensifications are their volitions that we can make room for praise and blame. Suppose that, as some neo-Lockeans hold, a self is just a sequence of mental events, among them volitions, and none with an owner other than that whole sequence. Then the value of the self would depend on the value of the whole sequence. Perhaps the whole sequence could at least be praised. Or suppose that, as Berkeley may have thought, the self, a Spirit, is a continuous willing rather than a sequence of discrete mental events. As he put it, 'Substance of a Spirit is that it acts, causes, wills, operates, or if you please (to avoid the quibble yt may be made on ye word it) to act, cause, will, operate'.[13] We could still evaluate the whole continuous process.

Actions I define in terms of volitions. They are either volitions, or things done by willing. Volitions I take to be events with a distinctive, introspectable quality. They form a kind whose members include trying or making an effort, deciding, attending, judging or mentally assenting, and forming an intention. If it seems odd to deny that the sleeping man acted when he raised his arm, or that her fidgeting was an action, unconscious or abstracted though it was, then allow that actions can include movements of a kind some instances of which are willed. Distinguish, if you like, between actions in the central sense, which are either volitions, or done by willing, and actions in the peripheral sense, which are movements of a kind some instances of which are willed.

At least some of us are at least sometimes active. Perhaps not all of us, because to will you must be conscious, must think of what you will, and, as noted in section 1.3, a forever unconscious entity, which thinks of nothing, can with selfhood taken as I define it still be a self. It may exist for a time with the right constant quality to be a self, but then be destroyed without ever having become conscious. While it exists, it may still be one of us.

To will you must be conscious. To function as an agent, you must function as a subject. Can you function as a subject without functioning as an agent? Perhaps not. Perhaps, as Kant maintained, there can be no consciousness without a unifying activity.[14] Non-human animals may be different. They may have sometimes conscious but never active selves. Maybe bees and worms have selves which think, and have wants and experiences, but whose constant qualities are never intensified into any of those events which I called volitions. It is supposed by some panpsychists that there are entities which compose material objects and are analogous to human selves. These analogous entities I call ulterior selves. Perhaps they too are never active. I shall say no more about the selves of non-human animals. Some arguments for the existence of ulterior selves will be considered in Chapter 2.

1.5 Disseveralities

Selves, as I define them, are enduring substances of which this is true: for each, there is a single quality, which is its constant possession, which it does not share with any other substance, and which, if not remembered by it as its own, still has an affinity with a quality which some self remembers having had. And, I affirm, *we* are selves, as so defined. By a substance, I mean an independent entity which has properties. In the section after this one, more will be said about substances as so conceived. But let me assume for the moment that we are substances. So far, I have maintained that each of us has a constantly possessed quality, either revealed by memory or akin to a quality which someone's memory has revealed. Such a quality I will call *ipseical*, and a substance with an ipseical quality I will call an *ipseity*. An ipseical quality which is possessed by no more than one substance, I will call a *disseveral* quality, and a substance with a disseveral quality, I will call a *disseverality*. I maintain, then, that we are disseveralities.

I do not at all deny that there are affinities between different disseveral qualities. There may indeed be groups of disseveral qualities whose members have an affinity with each other closer than the affinity which any member has to any non-member of the group. Affinities between disseveral qualities may bear a certain resemblance to the kinships between the different determinates of a single determinable colour, such as those as between scarlet, crimson, russet, vermilion, ..., all determinates of red. But there are more of us than there are determinates of any determinable colour, more of us, even, than there are determinates of all the determinable colours put together. Echoing Edith Stein, one might compare our disseveral qualities with the leaves and blooms in an immeasurably variegated *Kranz*.[15] Disseveral qualities are in fact not easy to distinguish from the individual forms on whose existence the saint insisted in her courageous *Auseinandersetzung* with the Thomist theory of a common human nature individuated just by matter.

That we are disseveralities is a centrally important feature of what we are. And that selves are disseveralities is vital as well to the argument which I will advance in Chapter 3 for the existence of at least one transcendent self. According to that argument, it is only by the activity of at least one transcendent self that the existence of all nonselves of a certain kind can be explained. But that will be true only if no nonself of that kind explains the existence of the explanatory transcendent self or selves. And, as we will see, that condition will be fulfilled if and only if transcendent selves are disseveralities.

Stronger than the thesis that we each have an ipseical quality not shared with any other substance is the thesis that we each have an ipseical quality not shared with any other particular. There are philosophers of perception who suppose that when you have a visual experience as of a scarlet poppy, you are related to a scarlet sense datum. As I define a substance, a sense datum is not a substance. It lacks the necessary independence. A sense datum cannot exist unless there is someone to whom it is given. If your experience as of a scarlet poppy is veridical, then on the sense datum theory, there is a non-substantial particular which shares the quality scarlet with an independently existing poppy: this particular is the sense datum. Assume for the moment the sense datum theory and suppose that you have a veridical memory of having a visual experience as of a scarlet poppy. Is there then a dependent particular, analogous to a sense datum, with which you share a quality? Suppose there is. Will you not in that case be a particular with a quality shared only with those other particulars which are the data presented by your own memories of yourself? Not necessarily. Of his 'selfbeing', Hopkins wrote not just that it had a taste 'more distinctive than the taste of ale or alum, more distinctive than the smell of walnut leaf or camphor', but also that it was 'incommunicable by any means to any other man...Searching nature I taste *self* but at one tankard, that of my own being'.[16] But is it not possible that even on this side of the grave you may have a veridical awareness of the ipseical quality of another self? If so, then this other self will have an ipseical quality which is shared not only with the particulars which are the data presented by its own memory of itself but also with the particular which is the datum presented by your awareness of this other self. But let me return from these niceties to the thesis that if we are substances, then we each have an ipseical quality unshared with any other substance. Let me return to the thesis that if we are substances, then we are disseveralities. Why is *that* to be believed?

It is to be believed because we are many, and by the principle of the Identity of Indiscernibles, no two of us have all the same properties, and the simplest unfalsified hypothesis about how in every pair of us one of us has a property which the other does not have is that in every pair of us each of us has a different ipseical quality.

From now onwards, I will refer to the Identity of Indiscernibles as the Dissimilarity of the Diverse, or for short DD.[17] DD has of course been challenged, most famously by Max Black's thought experiment about a universe containing nothing but two exactly similar pure iron spheres.[18] Of the much that has been said against the DD principle, I will consider only Richard Swinburne's claim that different particulars may differ not in their properties but just in their 'thisness'. According to Swinburne, 'A substance has thisness iff there could exist instead of it (or in addition to it) a different substance which has all the same properties as it, monadic and relational'.[19] He invites us to imagine 'a world in which you have this body and I that one (and the mental life connected with that); and a world in which you have that body (and the mental life connected with that) and I have this one'. There is, he thinks, an evident difference between the two worlds. 'What could be more obvious?... And yet unless you and I both have thisness, something other than our properties which makes us the people that we are, these two worlds would be the same'.[20] A fuller version of this rather compressed reasoning might go as follows. Let M* denote the conjunction of my mental properties, P* the conjunction of my physical properties, M+ the conjunction of your mental properties and P+ the conjunction of your physical properties. Let A denote a possible world in which I exist with M* and P* and you exist with M+ and P+, and let B denote a possible world in which I exist with M+ and P+ and you exist with M* and P*. There is an evident difference between the two possible worlds A and B. The difference cannot lie in the properties which are instantiated in the two possible worlds. For in both possible worlds, the same properties are instantiated, namely M*, P*, M+ and P+. How else can the two possible worlds differ? It could be that (i) in A there is an individual with M* and P*, and in B there is a different individual with M* and P*, or it could be that (ii) in A there is an individual with M+ and P+ and in B there is a different individual with M+ and P+. Consider (i). If the individual in A which has M* and P* is different from the individual in B which has M* and P*, then the difference between these two individuals cannot be that they have different properties. For they both have the same properties, namely M* and P*. We can call the residual difference between the two individuals a difference in their thisnesses. Similar reasoning applies to (ii). If the individual in B which has M+ and P+ is different from the individual in B which has M+ and P+, then the difference between these two individuals cannot be that they have different properties. For they both have the same properties, namely M+ and P+. Here again the residual difference between the two individuals can be called a difference in their thisnesses.

I do not think that this argument undermines DD. The most that the argument shows is that there are possible worlds in which different individuals have the same properties. But from that nothing follows about the actual world. Nothing more follows than that DD is not a necessary truth. For all that the argument shows, DD may still be a contingent truth. And there is a further difficulty with the argument. Of any entity to which properties are ascribed one can ask, What, as distinct from its properties, is the entity itself? An attractive answer to the question is that it is based on a false assumption. Actually, there are no such things as properties and the entities which have them: there are, rather, sets or sums of exactly resembling particulars, and swarms or bundles of diverse but concurrent or compresent particulars. But this particularist answer is not available when we ask the question, what, as distinct from its properties, is an entity with thisness? Take the individual in A which has M* and P* and suppose that there is another individual in B which has the same properties. We cannot give a particularist answer to the question, What is the individual in A? which is different from a particularist answer to the question, What is the individual in B?

We are many. By the principle of the Dissimilarity of the Diverse, no two of us have all the same properties. We each have an ipseical quality. And the simplest unfalsified hypothesis about how in every any pair of us one has a property which the other does not have is that in any pair of us each of us has a different ipseical quality. What other hypotheses suggest themselves? Might it be that in any pair of us one of us has a mental property that the other lacks? Or perhaps that in any pair of us, one of us has a causal property that the other lacks, a property for example of causing or being caused by an event in some body to events in which the other member of the pair is not causally related? Or perhaps that in any pair of us, one of the two has a spatial property that the other lacks? I will maintain that all of these alternative hypotheses must be rejected. A disjunctive hypothesis may now suggest itself, namely that in any pair of us either one of us has a mental property that the other lacks, or one of us has a causal property that the other lacks, or one of us has a spatial property that the other lacks. But the difficulty with this suggestion is that precisely because it is disjunctive, this hypothesis is more complex than the non-disjunctive hypothesis of our disseverality to which it is supposed to be a more acceptable alternative.

First, then, the hypothesis that in every pair of us, one member of the pair has a mental property that the other member lacks. To this, there are two objections. The first is that for all we know, there are pairs of us in which neither member has any mental property at all. There may be pairs of us in which both members are unconscious, not just in the sense that they are not aware that they are thinking or willing this or that and cannot without some form of therapy come to that awareness, but rather in the sense that neither has any mental life at all. Ipseical qualities are not mental properties. To have a mental property is to be conscious of something, and an entity can have an ipseical quality without being conscious of anything. It is necessary only that it has a quality akin to a one which some self remembers having had. It may perfectly well be that you had an ipseical quality before you had a body and the mental life which events in that body caused. The other objection to the hypothesis that in every pair of us one member of the pair has a mental property that the other member lacks is that there can be pairs of us in which the only mental property possessed by either member of the pair is a property which the two members share. So, for example it can be that the only mental property possessed by either member of the pair is an awareness of exactly the same patch of blue.

Next, the hypothesis that in any pair of us, one of us has a causal property that the other lacks. The most plausible version of this hypothesis is that in every pair of us, one of us has a body that the other member lacks, which is to say, for any pair of us, there is a body events in which either cause or are caused by mental events which depend on one member of the pair but not on the other member of the pair. There is a subtle objection to this version of the causal hypothesis, an objection which invokes what has become known as the Problem of Causal Pairings. It is that on a certain conception of causality, we cannot tell which member of the pair it is that has the body to which the other member is supposed not to be causally related. But I will defer what I have to say against this causal pairings objection until I come to section 1.7, in which I uphold the thesis that at least some of us are in at least some phases of our existence embodied. A simpler objection is that for all we know, there are times at which, in some pairs of us, *neither* member of the pair has a body. The evidence reviewed by C.D. Broad in his *Lectures on Psychical Research* led him to admit that he would be slightly more annoyed than surprised should he find himself in some sense persisting immediately after the death of his present body.[21] We too may suspect there will be or even was a time at which in at least some pairs of us, both members are entirely bodiless. We have bodies now, but it is paradoxical to say that we are distinguished from each other by what for all we know distinguishes us from each other only now. Can you so much as conceive that you exist without a body? As Descartes insisted, no contradiction is entailed by 'I am thinking and I have no body', and if, unlike Descartes, one affirms not only that the I is an unknown thinker, but that the I has an ipseical quality, one will be in a better position than Descartes was to deny that any contradiction is entailed.

Finally, the hypothesis that in any pair of us, one member has a spatial property that the other lacks. The most plausible version of this hypothesis is that for any pair of us, there is a point in space or region of space at or in which just one member of the pair is located. Philosophers have constructed arguments which if sound would show that there is no real space in which anything is located. And if neither member of the pair has a spatial location, then their spatial locations are not different. The thought is that no space exists independently of whether or not anyone has experiences of shapes and sizes or of distances between objects. There is a phenomenal space in which some of the objects as of which you have experiences appear to be located. It may appear to you that a patch of red is to the left of a patch of blue, even if no patches of colour exist independently of your experience, or even if no patches of colour which exist independently of your experience are really at distances from each other. Perhaps it is true that 'experiential contents of whatever type can only seem to be presented to a subject if that subject has the impression of being itself spatially related to what it perceives'.[22] But there is no real space. Either space is as Kant maintained transcendentally ideal, or, alternatively, and as has also been argued, space is part of a 'world-suggestive system of appearance... ordained and authorised by God'.[23] I suspend judgement on these idealist arguments. I suggest, however, although there may be a real space in which human brains and bodies are located, we would not be located in this space, unless, what is not the case, we are identical to bodies or brains or parts of them. And if none of us is spatially located, then it is not the case that in any pair of us one member of the pair has a spatial location that the other member lacks.

Why is it not the case that we are identical to brains or bodies or parts of them? It has been said that if this were the case, then it would be impossible to account for your identity over time. If you exist at time t1 and are a brain or part of one, then what makes you the same person as a person who exists at time t2? The answer will presumably depend on how much of the brain or brain part or part of it which you were t1 continues to exist at t2. But there will always be borderline cases, in which the answer to the question of whether you exist at t2 will be quite arbitrary. Do you exist at time t2 only if at least 51 percent of your time t1 brain or brain part still exists at time t2, or only if at least 52 percent of it still exists? There is no yes or no answer to the question. But there must be a yes or no answer to the question. So, you are not a brain or part of a brain. The argument is unconvincing. Why must there be a yes or no answer to the question of how much of the brain or part of it that you were at t continues to exist at t2? How do we know that even if our language does suggest that there is always such an answer our language is not misleading?

But there is a better objection to the theory that we are identical to brains or parts of brains. It is that the theory collides with what we know about the unity of consciousness.[24] Sometimes when functioning as a subject, one will be aware of what is presented to one as a unified visual field, a unified complex. For the subject to have this awareness not for it to have proper parts, each of which is aware of some part of the whole field. An entity which is not a proper part of the subject but is rather the whole subject is aware of the whole visual field, the whole unified complex. Is the whole something which thus functions as a subject itself a complex? No, because the properties of a complex are reducible to the properties and relations of its parts, and the whole subject has a property, namely its awareness of the unified complex, such that there are no parts of the subject to whose awarenesses the subject's own awareness of the unified visual complex is reducible, and no parts of the subject to the relations between which the subject's own awareness of the unified complex is reducible. Could the whole subject be a brain or part of a brain? No, because both brains and parts of brains are complexes and the whole subject is not a complex. So, if the subject has a real spatial location only if it is a brain or part of a brain, then it has no real spatial location. Put more formally, the argument is this.

(1) Brains and parts of brains are complexes
(2) The properties of a complex are reducible to the properties of and relations between their parts

16 *Human Selves*

(3) Sometimes you are aware of a whole visual field
(4) If you are aware of a whole visual field, then you have a property which is not reducible to the properties of and relations between your parts
(5) You are not a complex (from 2, 3 and 4)
(6) You are neither a brain nor a part of a brain (from 1 and 5)

(1) – (6) should be distinguished from an argument about the unity of consciousness which takes the case in which a subject is presented with a state of consciousness in which experiences of different modalities are combined, a state, say, in which the hearing of a chord on an organ is combined with the sight of a rose window. The thought here is that if the subject were a brain or part of a brain, then we would have to say that its visual experience is fully located in one neural region, and its auditory experience fully located in another neural region, and this would be incompatible with the unity of the subject's experience. The visual experience and the auditory experience would not be states of the same entity, and they would not possess a conjoint phenomenal character. As Tim Bayne has pointed out, this argument relies on the popular but unjustified assumption that if a subject is a brain or part of a brain, then its modality-specific experiences are indeed 'fully located in discrete regions of neural space'.[25]

Is the argument (1) – (6) outweighed by some other argument whose conclusion is that we are indeed identical to brains or parts of them? It is often claimed that only if we accept that we are identical to brains or parts of them can we avoid the 'formality and emptiness', the 'fatal thinness' of the Cartesian theory of the self as a thinking substance. Only then can we give some positive answer to the question of what, as distinct from its thinking, is the thing that thinks, and avoid the Hobbesian charge of reifying an attribute. But the thinness is avoided just by the supposition that we have ipseical qualities.

We may be reminded that

> The standard view [until the time of Descartes] had the soul located in its entirety at every point in space occupied by its physical body. The idea is that souls and bodies both occupy space but they do so in different ways. Bodies occupy space by virtue of their substantive parts occupying subregions of the space occupied by the complex whole. Because souls have no separable parts, they must be present in their entirety at every point in the space that they occupy. The upshot is that souls, while having no shape themselves, occupy shaped regions of space. And because souls and bodies occupy space in different ways, they can occupy the same space ... the soul occupies the space occupied by its physical body because that is the space it seems to occupy. For example, when your foot is stepped on, you feel pain *in your foot*. And when your head is hit, you feel pain *in your head*. You, your entirety,

feel the pains in these places *simultaneously*, so that you must be present in your entirety and at the same time in your foot and in your head. Furthermore, even without feeling these pains when and where you feel them, you feel like you occupy the space of your body. You feel right now as if you are simultaneously in your arms, legs, head,...The term for the capacity for you to feel in this way is 'proprioception'.[26]

On a scholastic conception of souls as substantial forms of bodies, the space occupied by your soul is different from the space occupied by mine. But to say that I have an ipseical quality is not to say that my body has a substantial form. Perhaps it is true that experiential contents of certain types can only seem to be presented to a subject if that subject has an impression of being spatially related to what it is perceiving. The subject is related in its phenomenal space to what it is perceiving. But I do not accept that even in its phenomenal space, the subject is in the same place as what it is perceiving. If I feel a pain in my foot, I have the impression that the subject of the experience is behind my eyes, and between my ears. But even if I have the impression that there is a pain in my foot, I do not have the impression that the subject of the experience, that which feels the pain, is in my foot.

With selfhood taken as I define it, we are selves only if we are disseveralities, substances each with an ipseical quality possessed by just one substance. I have defended the principle of the Dissimilarity of the Diverse and have argued that the simplest answer to the question of what makes any pair of us conform to this principle is that each member of the pair has a different ipseical quality. With selfhood taken as I define it, we are selves only if we are substances. In the next section, I say more about substances.

1.6 Substances

A substance has been defined as an individual object (Aristotle's 'first substance'), as the nature of something (Aristotle's 'second substance'), as that of which things can be predicated but which cannot be predicated of anything else, as a system of parts so organised that the continued existence of the whole is dependent on the cooperation of the parts, as an independent entity.[27] By a substance I shall mean an entity both independent and possessed of properties. Are we in this sense substances?

Only if there are entities which have properties. What is it for an entity to have a property? One answer is to reject the question: we should be thinking not of properties and entities which have them but rather just of different kinds of sets or sums of particulars. The universal property red can be reduced to a set or sum of exactly resembling particulars, to a set or sum of exactly resembling rednesses. And entities which have several universal properties can be reduced to swarms or bundles of diverse but concurrent or compresent particulars. If a post box is red, then it is a bundle of particulars which includes a particular redness. The particulars which form these swarms or bundles are often called tropes, an arbitrary name introduced by Donald Williams.[28] But though a simple tropist answer is available to the question of what it is for a post box to be red, there does not seem to be a simple tropist answer to the question about it is for an entity to have a disseveral quality. Since disseveral qualities are unshared, there will be no swarm of exactly resembling particulars to which a disseveral quality is reducible, or swarm of diverse particulars to which the disseverality which has the quality is reducible. We may favour an ontology in which all shared or universal properties are reducible to sets or sums of tropes. But if we do, we will have to qualify the view that tropes are, as Donald Williams put it 'the primary constituents of this and any other possible world, the very alphabet of being'. Williams himself acknowledged that they would be the primary constituents only if 'a whole soul or mind...is not an immaterial substance on its own'.[29] But in the rest of the book, I will continue to talk of properties, and leave the reader who so wishes to make his own translation into an ontology which if not fully tropist is at least purely particularist.

What does it mean to say that substances are independent entities? Should we define 'independent' so that an entity x is independent only if there is no other entity y, apart from one of x's essential proper parts and apart from an essential property of x, such that it is impossible that x exists and y does not exist? No, because then we would have to say that you are not a substance. If y's non-existence is impossible, and y is neither one of x's essential parts nor an essential property of x, then whatever entity x stands for, it will be impossible that both x exists and y does not exist. And if a substance is an independent entity, and if there is an entity, such as the number 5, whose non-existence is impossible and which is neither one of your essential parts nor one of your essential properties, then on the suggested definition of independence you are not a substance.

Let me say, then, that an entity x is independent if and only if for every other entity y *whose non-existence is possible*, and which is neither an essential property of x nor one of x's essential proper parts, it is possible that x exists and y does not. You are a substance, I now maintain, because for everything other than you whose non-existence is possible and which is neither one of your essential properties nor one of your essential proper parts, it is possible that you exist and it does not. Intentional contents are by contrast non-substances. They depend for their existence on the subjects of whose conscious states they are the contents, and they are neither parts nor properties of those subjects.

What, in all this, is 'possible' supposed to mean? I do not take it as a primitive modal term. 'It is possible both that x exists and y does not exist'

I take to mean '"x exists and y does not exist" is intelligible', and the latter I take to mean 'It is not the case that were anyone to try to understand "x exists and y does not exist" then he would fail'. How should we interpret 'Were anyone to try to understand "x exists and y does not exist" then he would fail'? I think we should take its assertion as a convenient way of asserting that everyone who tries to understand "x exists and y does not exist" fails. Whether an entity has the independence necessary for it to be a substance depends, then, on our psychology. But that does not imply that whether an entity is a substance lies somehow within our control. Suppose that 'something is (positively) valuable if and only we would be disposed under conditions of the fullest possible imaginative acquaintance to desire to desire it'.[30] Then whether an object has positive value depends on our psychology, as it would not so depend if positive value were, say, a simple non-natural property. But that which under conditions of the fullest imaginative acquaintance we would desire to desire is not something that we are free to determine as we wish. Nor are we free to determine the limits of intelligibility.

I think, then, that in an independence-dependent sense, we are substances, and since we each have a disseveral quality, an ipseical quality possessed by no more than one substance, we are disseveralities, and hence selves. A self may be either transcendent or non-transcendent, and if non-transcendent, it may or may not be an ulterior self. It is transcendent if it causes both the existence of any non-abstract nonselves there may be which are not composed of selves, and the existence of all those selves which do not cause the existence of every other self. It is ulterior if it is a component of a material object. We are non-transcendent, and as I will later maintain, non-ulterior selves. So also, if they exist, are angels, and the selves of higher animals. In the next two sections, on embodiment and freedom, I say more about the kind of selves we are. But first, something more about 'possible' in my definition of independence.

According to this definition, an entity x is independent if and only if for every other entity y whose non-existence is possible, and which is neither an essential property of x nor one of x's essential proper parts, it is possible that x exists and y does not. And for 'possible', in this definition, I offered a psychological analysis. Would it not be better to take it as a primitive modal term, meaningful albeit indefinable in any but other modal terms? I think not.

We may be tempted to deny that there are *any* primitive and meaningful modal terms. Empirical Atomism is a developed version of Hume's concept empiricism. It 'takes the basic units of meaning to be primitive (not further analysable) concepts, restricts genuine primitive concepts to ones which are, in some paradigmatic sense, empirical (e.g. ones which can be grasped ostensively), acknowledges other genuine concepts only if they can be analysed into such primitive concepts, and thus restricts genuine propositions to ones which are composed exclusively of concepts whose genuineness is empirically certified in this way'.[31] The Empirical Atomist need not suppose that all significant primitive words ...are ostensively definable in a sense which requires the subject mentally to select 'some component or aspect of what is, for him currently, experientially given...and stipulate that the word is to signify ...that selected item. ... For some of the primitive words will be terms drawn from the apparatus of formal logic - terms such as "and", "not", "some", and "any", as well as the auxiliary devices of variables and brackets'. He can retain the principle that all significant primitive terms are ostensively definable, whilst broadening his conception of the ostensive procedure by which their meanings are fixed or revealed. 'Thus while a logical term such as "and" does not, on its own, signify something which could be an element of the given, there are sentences which do - sentences, such as "this is red and round", which can be used to report some state of affairs which is directly experienced'. The word "and" does have indirectly an ostensible meaning, via the ostensible meaning of such sentences'.[32] We can ostensively define the word by indicating the types of experience which conclusively verify its use in certain sentential contexts. 'Moreover, it becomes clear... that a similar procedure is required for the ostensive definition of *any* word. Even if we choose an explicitly phenomenal word, such as "blue", we cannot fully specify its meaning by associating it, in isolation, with some element of the given. For the full meaning of "blue", just because it embodies the contribution of that word to the meaning of any sentence containing it, includes its grammatical category, and this is not something that we can indicate ostensively except via its use in sentential contexts'.[33] It is also necessary to emphasise the distinction between Empirical Atomism and the verificationism of the logical positivists: 'even if the meanings of the primitive words are determined by the methods of verifying certain sentences containing them, it does not follow that *all* significant sentences are verifiable, much less that the meaning of a sentence is contained in its method of verification'.[34] Empirical Atomism is an attractive doctrine, and it could seem that given Empirical Atomism, and given that we lack the experiences as of modality which would allow us an ostensive grasp of modal concepts, we must conclude that there are no meaningful primitive modal terms.

The conclusion is too sweeping. There is one kind of modality of which we do have experience. Often, one has an experience of what can be called one's own volitional power. Often one has an experience of being both able, in one's present circumstances, to decide to A, and able, in those same circumstances, to decide not to A. And, as I shall maintain when in section 1.8 I come to discuss our freedom, the concept of this two-way ability is primitive and unanalysable: 'able', in this context, is a meaningful primitive modal term. Yet although there are experiences that allow the modal terms which stand for a self's two-way volitional ability to be at once meaningful and primitive, there seem not to be any experiences which would give that status to 'possible', as it figures in my definition of substantial independence.

But for the moment, I will say no more about primitive modality. More will be said in section 3.6 and in Excursus A. I turn now to the topic of our embodiment.

1.7 Embodied

We are selves. And at least some of us are in at least some phases or periods of our existence embodied. Why 'at least some of us'? Why not affirm that *all* of us are in at least some phases or periods of our existence embodied? Why indeed not affirm that we are compounds of selves and bodies? Because with selfhood taken as I define it, a self might exist and then be destroyed without ever coming to have a body, and it would then still have been one of us. If a self has a body in some period of its existence, must it always have a body? Not at all. With selfhood taken as I defined it, a self may for all we know survive the destruction or disintegration of its body. It might for all we know survive the destruction of its body either in the womb, or after it has been born. It might for all we know survive the eventual disintegration of its body in extreme old age. If one is a compound of a self and a body, then for all we know one may come to be identical to what was previously only a part of one, which is absurd.[35]

A self is embodied only if there is a causal relation between a body and mental events which belong to and hence depend on that self. Though a self can be conscious without being embodied, the converse does not hold. The causal relation between the mental events and the body must be direct, in the sense that x is a direct cause of y if and only if x causes y and if another event causes y it does so only by causing x. A self S is embodied if and only if (i) there is one and only one body events in which are sometimes directly causally related to mental events dependent on S, and (ii) S is the only self whose dependent mental events are sometimes directly causally related to events belonging to that body. Each embodied self owns just one body, and no body is owned by more than one embodied self.

But what is a body? For the commonsense realist a body is, like any other material object, pretty much as it appears to be. There is no great difference between what it appears to be and what really, or in itself, it is. For the commonsense realist, a material object is, as it appears to be, 'a three – dimensional solid filled with coloured stuff of some sort'.[36] But for the scientific realist, the commonsense conception of the material world has been totally undermined by modern physics. For the scientific realist, our experiences as of bodies are caused by entities postulated by scientific theories, and these entities do not closely or at all resemble the contents of the appearances which they cause us to enjoy. For some scientific realists, our experiences as of spatially located bricks and trees, or as of spatially located brains and arms and legs, are caused not by elementary particles but rather by 'patterns of activity in various space-filling quantum fields'.[37] It has been said that the explanatory entities of modern physics are 'almost inconceivably insubstantial relative to our everyday conception of material objects. They are "mere" collocations of patterns of energy, fabulously diaphanous process entities whose existence involves a constant interchange with the quantum vacuum, given which it is literally correct to say that they're partly constituted by the vacuum'.[38] They are 'quite astoundingly insubstantial', 'an intricately shimmering almost-nothing'.[39] However this may be, scientific realists divide into those who hold that the explanatory entities postulated by scientific theories have non-relational properties, and those who hold that they are just relations.[40] Of those who think that the explanatory entities have non-relational properties, some think that science itself gives us knowledge only of the relational properties of these entities. Those who think that the explanatory entities are just relations divide into those who think that the relations are spatial, and those who think that they are purely mathematical. And of those scientific realists who think that while the explanatory entities have non-relational properties, science gives us knowledge only of their relational properties, some think that the scientifically known relational properties are spatial, others that they are purely mathematical. That the explanatory entities have non-relational properties is consistent with the doctrine that in themselves these entities are extended substances on which a relational space depends. But it is also consistent with the doctrine that these entities are aggregates of non-spatial selves.

The realist doctrine that scientific theories provide us with knowledge of explanatory entities is of course to be distinguished from the instrumentalist doctrine that they provide us just with ways to order and predict the contents of our experiences. Some instrumentalists affirm, with Berkeley, that no material objects exist which are not mere contents of human or divine thoughts or experiences. Others affirm, with Kant, that our experiences as of material objects are explained by our own mental operations on what is supplied to us by an unknown but independently existing *Ding an sich*. On a neo-Kantian or Duhemian view of science, scientific theories provide us just with ways to order and predict our experiences as of the material world, and the unobservable objects of which scientific theories speak have no existence which is independent of our experience. As Poincaré says somewhere, 'the gross matter furnished us by our sensations is but a crutch for our infirmity'. But on a neo-Kantian or Duhemian view of science, bodies, as they are in themselves, might still for all we know be much as they appear to be.

It could seem that if it is part of the definition of a self's embodiment that there is just one body events in which are directly causally related to mental events dependent on that self, and just one self whose dependent mental events are directly causally related to events belonging to that body, then a self might fail to be embodied because there is no such double exclusivity. A self might fail to be embodied because more than one body is directly causally related to mental events dependent on that self, or because this self is not the only self whose dependent mental events are directly causally related to a given body. That there are cases of the second kind may seem to be supported by observations of so-called multiple personality, or of the effects of split-brain operations which appear to have destroyed a patient's unity of consciousness. But perhaps such observations can be explained away.[41] Also to be considered is the kind of thought-experiment, which for all I know may become a reality, in which half of self X's brain is destroyed, and half of self Y's brain is destroyed, and the remaining half of self X's brain is transplanted into the place below Y's skull which was previously occupied by the now destroyed half of Y's brain. Are we to say that X and Y continue to exist as separate selves and that mental events dependent on each now stand direct causal relations to the one composite brain which now exists below Y's skull? In that case we will have to say that neither self is embodied, as embodiment has been defined. But that is not the only option. Perhaps X and Y cease to have disseveral qualities, and so cease to be selves, as selfhood has been defined.

A self is embodied only if there is a body events in which stand in a direct causal relation to mental events which belong to that self, where x is a direct cause of y if and only if x causes y, and if another event causes y it does so only by causing x. Consistently with this general condition, a self might be embodied either (A) in the sense that there is a body some events in which are directly caused by some mental events belonging to that self, or (B) in the sense that there is a body events in which directly cause some mental events belonging to that self, or even (C) in the sense that there is or has been a body by events in which all subsequent mental events belonging to that self are caused. It is hard not to believe that at least some of us are at least sometimes embodied in senses (A) and (B), hard enough, I think, for the onus to lie on anyone who disputes its truth. I will criticise what seem to be the most plausible of the arguments which philosophers have constructed against the doctrine that at least some of us are at least sometimes embodied in sense (A). I have not found any objections worth criticising to the claim that at least some of us are at least sometimes embodied in sense (B). What of sense (C)? I will do no more than raise a few doubts about what seem to be the most plausible arguments against our being in that sense embodied. A question now arises that I am wholly incompetent to pursue. I mean the question of whether a coherent interpretation of quantum theory can be found which does not postulate a form of psycho-physical interaction which entails (A). For all I know, there is no coherent interpretation of quantum theory which does not postulate the physical efficacy of attempts to measure physical quantities, or even, as with many-worlds interpretations of quantum theory, the cosmos-splitting efficacy of such attempts.

Embodiment in sense (A)

A self is embodied in sense (A) if there is a body some events in which are directly caused by mental events belonging to that self. Mental events I take to include volitions: I take them to include those actions whose intimate relation to the self which consists in their being intensifications of the self's ipseical and disseveral quality.[42] A familiar argument against our embodiment in sense (A) goes as follows.

(1) Mental events are not identical to physical events
(2) Every bodily event has an immediate sufficient physical cause
(3) No bodily event is overdetermined
(4) So no mental event is the direct cause of any bodily event.

This argument offers a conspicuous hostage to fortune in the shape of premise (2), otherwise known as the principle of the Causal Closure of the Physical (CCP). Here is what is perhaps the best that can be said for CCP.

> '...during the late nineteenth and the twentieth centuries an increasing number of scientists have come to doubt the existence of vital and mental forces. The most significant evidence seems to have come directly from physiology and molecular biology rather than from physics. Over the last hundred and fifty years a great deal has come to be known about the workings of biological systems (including brains), and there has been no indication that anything other than basic physical forces is needed for their operation. In particular, the twentieth century has seen an explosion of knowledge about processes occurring within cells, and here too there is no evidence other than the familiar physical chemistry. The result has been that the overwhelming majority of scientists now reject vital and mental forces, and accept the causal closure of the physical realm'.[43]

The thought is that the principle is made probable by the ever-increasing number of accepted scientific laws which without mentioning mental conditions for the occurrence of physical events give physical conditions for the occurrence of such events. It may not a good objection to CCP that it is falsified by quantum indeterminacy. On some interpretations, quantum mechanics still specifies that random physical effects have their probabilities fixed by sufficient immediate physical causes. CCP could be understood as covering this kind of physical determination of physical probabilities.[44]

There is however a strong and obvious objection to CCP. That a scientific law does not mention mental conditions for the occurrence of physical events does not mean that there are no such conditions. The law may be intended to apply only in contexts in which such mental conditions will not be present. There are in fact plausible accounts of the general relations between experience and scientific theory on which it would, for this reason, be quite erroneous to infer CCP from what we know of physics. One such account has been provided by Stephan Körner. According to Körner, scientific theories are idealizations of experience, by deductive unification and deductive abstraction. Idealization by deductive unification eliminates mental predicates from physical theories 'because the elementary classical logic underlying all physical theories is extensional and thus does not accommodate any intentional predicates, such as that of being confronted with alternative courses of action one of which may be a figment of the imagination'. Idealization by deductive abstraction eliminates mental predicates 'because the ideal individuals to which the various physical theories refer—particles, fields and the like—are conceived and postulated as possessing certain physical characteristics only, and no mental characteristics at all'. But the absence within a physical theory 'of any reference to mental events and characteristics, and thus to choices, does not imply their absence, their physical ineffectiveness or their dependence within the extra-theoretical world, especially not in those contexts in which no identification of theoretical predicates is intended'.[45]

'Physics does not after all imply, and physicists, qua physicists, do not hold, that physically effective ...choices never change the course of events. Rather, they hold only that physical theory applies, and is to be applied, to situations in which such choices do not occur or, at least, are negligible. It is metaphysicians who seem to argue from the applicability of physical theories in choice-free situations to the physical ineffectiveness...of all choices. If dogmatic behaviourists are like people who argue that since winter coats are not used in summer, they do not exist, "physicalists" are like people who argue that since winter coats are not used in summer, they give no protection against the winter cold'.[46]

Other arguments against the sense (A) embodiment of selves can perhaps be derived from the aspersions cast by Jaegwon Kim on interactionist mind-body dualism, aspersions cast on 'the possibility of immaterial souls, outside physical space, causally interacting with material objects in space'. If, as Kim thinks, there can be no causal interaction between immaterial souls and material objects in space, then you might think that it is equally impossible for a mental event to be the direct cause of a brain event.

According to Kim, the interactionist dualist owes us, but cannot provide, a principled explanation of why we should reject the following principle.

> (M*) It is metaphysically possible for there to be to be two souls, A and B, with the same intrinsic properties such that they both act in the same way at the same time and a change occurs in a material object C. But it is the action of A, not that of B, that is the cause of the change in C.

What pairing relation pairs the first soul, but not the second, with the material object? Since souls, as immaterial substances, are outside physical space and cannot bear spatial relations to anything, it is not possible to appeal to spatial relations to ground the pairing. What possible relations could provide causal pairings across the two domains, one of spatially located material things and the other of immaterial minds outside space?[47]

If the interactionist dualist can give a principled explanation of why it is 'metaphysically impossible' for there to be two souls with the same intrinsic properties, then this will also be a principled explanation of why we should reject (M*). And perhaps, if sense could be made of 'metaphysical possibility', the interactionist dualist could give us a principled explanation of why it is metaphysically impossible for there to be two souls with the same intrinsic properties. He might offer an analogue of the argument that I gave in section 1.5 for the thesis that selves are disseveralities. He might argue that each soul has an ipseical quality, and that the best way to reconcile the Dissimilarity of the Diverse with the existence of a plurality of souls is to maintain that no soul shares its ipseical quality with any other soul.

Kim has a further argument against interactionist dualism.

> There are two physical objects, P1 and P2, with the same intrinsic properties, and an action of an immaterial soul causally affects…P1 but not P2. Since P1 and P2 have identical intrinsic properties, they must have the same causal capacity ("passive" causal powers as well as "active" causal powers), and it would seem that the only way to make them discernible in a causal context is in their spatial relation to other things. Doesn't that mean that any pairing relation that can do the job must be a spatial relation? If so, the pairing problem for this case is insolvable since the soul is not in space and bears no spatial relation to anything. The soul cannot be any "nearer" to, or "more properly oriented toward," one physical object than another. Nor could we say that there was a causal barrier "between" the soul and one of the physical objects but not the other, for what could "between" mean as applied to something in space and something outside it? It remains a total mystery what nonspatial relations there could be that might help to distinguish, from the point of view of an immaterial soul, between two intrinsically indiscernible physical objects.[48]

The dualist should reply that he is concerned only with actualities and deny that there is any actual case of the kind here envisaged. He may insist that cases of the kind envisaged are excluded by what we might call the nomological principle, namely that where two events are causally related, their being so is wholly constituted by the way in which, via their non-causal properties and relations, they fall under some natural law or set of laws. Given this principle, and given that P1 and P2 have the same intrinsic properties, there is no way in which one and the same action can causally affect P1 but not P2.

Embodiment in senses (B) and (C)

A self is embodied in sense (B) if there is a body events in which cause some mental events belonging to that self, as when, according to the causal theory of perception, experiences as of scarlet poppies are sometimes caused, via the brain, by events in entities which bear some resemblance to the intentional contents of these experiences. A self is embodied in sense (C) if there is or has been a body by events in which all subsequent mental events belonging to that self are caused.

That sometimes at least we are embodied in sense (B) seems pretty obviously true. I do not know whether sometimes at least we are embodied in sense (C), and can do no more than express my doubts about some current arguments for the conclusion we never are. One of these arguments is about causal pairings; the other is about freedom.

Causal pairings

The nomological principle was that where two events are causally related, their being so is wholly constituted by the way in which, via their non-causal properties and relations, they fall under some natural law or set of laws. One might suppose that given the nomological principle and given that mental events are not spatially located there is no more reason to say, of some particular bodily event, that it is the direct cause of a mental event owned by one self rather than that it is the direct cause of a mental event owned by another self. That being so, one might be tempted to deny that we are ever embodied in sense (C). Consider this set of propositions.

(5) There is a pair of sense (C) embodied selves A and B
(6) A time t event in A's body is the direct cause of a mental event owned by A, but not the direct cause of a mental event owned by B
(7) A time t event in B's body is the direct cause of a mental event owned by B, but not the direct cause of a mental event owned by A
(8) Where two events are causally related, their being so is wholly constituted by the way in which, via their non-causal properties and relations, they fall under some natural law or set of laws
(9) Mental events are not spatially located
(10) The causal episode involving A is simultaneously duplicated by a causal episode involving B.

The propositions (5) – (10) cannot all be true. Which should go? (5) might seem the easiest to abandon.

28   *Human Selves*

The threat to sense (C) embodiment which seems to be posed by the inconsistency of the set (5) – (10) resembles the threat posed to Cartesian Dualism by an argument constructed and then criticised by John Foster. (8) is the same as the premise which in Foster's argument is called the nomological assumption.[49] In Foster's argument, the time t event in A's body is replaced by a time t neural event N which occurs in Smith's brain; the mental event owned by A is replaced by an experience E which occurs in Smith's mind a tenth of a second later; the time t event in B's body is replaced by a time t neural event N1 which occurs in Jones's brain; and the mental event owned by B is replaced by an experience E1 which occurs in Jones's mind a tenth of a second later. The natural law which, given the nomological assumption, we might initially take to account for the causal episode in Smith, is in Foster's argument of the following kind:

> L1: It is a law that whenever an event of physical type ϕ occurs in a brain of structural type Σ an experience of psychological type Ψ occurs a tenth of a second later

where it is understood that N is of type ϕ, that Smith's brain is of structural type Σ at t, and that E is of psychological type Ψ. To say that the causal episode in Smith is simultaneously duplicated in Jones will then be to say that

> Jones's brain is also of structural type Σ at t, that an event N' of type ϕ occurs in Jones's brain at t, and that N' directly causes, in Jones's mind a tenth of a second later, an experience E' of type Ψ. *Ex hypothesi*, N is the cause of E, and N' is the cause of E'. But these causal pairings would not be determined by the non-causal properties of the situation and the specified law. The only non-causal properties which are relevant to the law are: the ϕ-ness of N and N'; the Ψ-ness of E and E'; the structural character of the two brains; and the fact that N and N' occur, simultaneously, a tenth of a second before E and E'. Clearly, these factors, together with the law, do not determine which neural event is paired with which experiential event. They are neutral between the correct claim, that E is the effect of N, and E' the effect of N' and the incorrect claim, that E is the effect of N' and E' the effect of N.

> The inadequacy of L1 stems from the fact that it only links the specified physical type of event and the specified psychological type of event by means of a temporal relation ...The natural remedy would be to supplement the temporal relation with some further relation, so that, in combination, the two relations would link the physical and psychological items in a sufficiently determinate way – a way which would leave at most only one psychological relatum for each

physical event of the relevant type, and at most only one physical relatum for each psychological event of the relevant type. The question now becomes: what further relation is available to the dualist? Clearly the relation cannot be (as it is in the case of physical causation) spatial, since the dualist denies that mental events are genuinely located in space.

Foster does not think that there is any further relation whose combination with the temporal relation will link the neural and experiential items in a sufficiently determinate way. He does however offer the Cartesian Dualist two ways out. One is to ensure that psychophysical laws yield unique causal pairings by restricting their scope to particular persons.

Thus, for Smith and Jones, we could envisage the laws:

L (Smith): It is a law that whenever a ϕ-event occurs in brain Bs at a time when Bs is of structural type Σ, a Ψ-experience occurs a tenth of a second later in mind Ms

L (Jones): It is a law that whenever a ϕ-event occurs in brain Bj at a time when Bj is of structural type Σ, a Ψ-experience occurs a tenth of a second later in mind Mj

where Bs and Ms are respectively Smith's brain and mind, and Bj and Mj are respectively Jones's brain and mind.

The other way out that Foster offers is to reject what he calls the nomological assumption, the assumption that where two events are causally related, their standing in this relation is wholly constituted by the non-causal properties of the situation and the obtaining of certain covering laws.

If the believer in sense (C) embodiment faces essentially the same problem of causal pairings as the Cartesian Dualist, and if the Cartesian Dualist can avail himself of one or other of Foster's ways out, then perhaps that same way out will be available for the believer in sense (C) embodiment when he is confronted with the inconsistency of the set (5) – (10). At this point one may begin to wonder about the drawbacks of scope-restricted laws and about the truth-value of what Foster calls the nomological assumption.[50] I doubt, however, that when the believer in embodied selves is confronted by the inconsistency of the set (5) – (10), he must adopt either of Foster's ways out. I do not see why when confronted with the inconsistency of the set (5) – (10), the believer in sense (C) embodied selves cannot reject

(10) The causal episode in A is simultaneously duplicated by the causal episode in B.

It is of course conceivable that in circumstances like those described by (6) and (7) there is a simultaneous causal duplication of the kind that (10) postulates. But we do not have to accept (10) as a truth about what is actual, as distinct from merely possible. On the objection to his Causal Pairings argument against Dualism that the possibility of simultaneous duplications of causal episodes 'is too remote to be taken seriously', Foster replied that 'the mere fact that it is a *possibility* means as that the dualist needs to be able to accommodate it'.[51] I do not see why the dualist is under any such obligation. Why should he not be satisfied with actualities?

A self is embodied in sense (C) if there is or has been a body by events in which every subsequent mental event belonging to that self is caused. For the conclusion that we are never thus embodied, arguments of this form suggest themselves.

(1) Sometimes we act freely
(2) If a self acts freely, then its action is uncaused.
(3) So now it is not the case that for each mental event belonging to a self, there is or has been a body by events in which that mental event is caused.

This argument will be discussed in the next section.

We are non-transcendent selves and at least some of us are at least sometimes embodied, at least in senses (A) and (B). Are there any never embodied non-transcendent selves? Yes, if there are non-transcendent selves which exist for a time and are then destroyed before they acquire bodies. And yes, if there are angels. If angels exist then they are non-transcendent: no angel causes the existence of all selves which do not cause the existence of every other self. Nor do any angels have bodies, unless it was literally with an angel that Tobias wrestled. And perhaps no angel ever is destroyed. That there are angels is a doctrine taught by Judaism, Islam and Christianity and perhaps by other ostensibly revealed religions. Perhaps some sound argument exists for the truth of an ostensibly revealed religion which teaches that there are angels. But no such argument is offered here.

1.8 Free

With selfhood taken as I defined it, we are selves. Some of us are at least sometimes subjects. Some of us are at least sometimes agents as well as subjects, and in at least some periods of our existence embodied. I now maintain that sometimes when we are agents we act freely. Since decisions are a kind of actions, it is enough for it to be true that sometimes we act freely that sometimes we make free decisions. And that we sometimes make free decisions is the proposition on which I now focus. That sometimes we make decisions for which we are morally responsible, may be praised or blamed, is a different proposition, and not one which I shall discuss. I shall not, then, be considering Harry Frankfurt's famous thought-experiment, in which it is supposed that someone makes a morally responsible decision to do something despite the fact that he is robbed of the freedom not to make that decision by the existence of somebody else with the unexercised power to prevent him from making it.[52]

Sometimes I have an experience as of being both able, in my present circumstances, to decide to A, and able, in my present circumstances to decide not to A. And sometimes I have an experience as of being both able, in my present circumstances to decide to A, and able, in my present circumstances, not to decide to A. Both experiences are as of my having two not simultaneously realisable powers or abilities. Let me focus on the first experience, the experience as of being both able in my present circumstances to decide to A and able in my present circumstances to decide not to A. An example. Sitting in my orchard, I have an experience as of having both of two abilities. I have an experience as of being both now able to decide to get up and walk down to the sea and now able to decide not to get up and walk down to the sea. Suppose that my experience is veridical: it is an experience not just as of, but of, having the two abilities. Now suppose that immediately after having the veridical experience of having the two abilities, I decide to get up and walk down to the sea. What if I had instead decided not to get up and walk to the sea? Then, since it was a veridical experience that I had, the circumstances in which I would have made that decision would have been exactly the same as the circumstances in which I made my actual decision to get up and walk down to the sea. This has a bearing on the meaning of 'I was able to decide to A' and 'I was able to decide not to A'. One might have taken the latter to be analysable as a counterfactual conditional of the form 'If X had been the case I would have decided not to A'. But that cannot be right. For if, contrary to the facts, X had been the case, and I had then decided not to A, then, something would have been the case that in actuality was not the case, and then the circumstances of my decision not to A would *not* have been exactly the same as the actual circumstances in which I made my decision to A. And if 'I was able to decide not to A' cannot be analysed as a counterfactual of the form 'If X had been the case I would have decided not to A', then neither, presumably, can 'I was able to decide to A' be analysed as a conditional of the form 'If Y had been the case I would have decided to A.' Neither ability is analysable as a conditional. How then are the abilities to be analysed? The answer, I suggest, is that they are not analysable at all. They are primitive modalities, intelligible because experienced. In this they differ from the non-experienced and hence unintelligible primitive natural necessities which are sometimes supposed to link all causally related pairs of events, and whose existence I rejected in section 1.6.

By a free decision to A, I shall mean a decision to A which someone makes straight after he has had a veridical experience either as of being both able to decide to A and in exactly the same circumstances able not to decide to A, or a veridical experience as of being both able not to decide to A and in exactly the same circumstances able to decide to A.

With 'free decision' so understood, do we sometimes make free decisions? Against the occurrence of free decisions as so understood, it might be said either (a) we never have experiences even as of having the required two abilities, or (b) although we do sometimes have experiences as of having the required two abilities, such experiences are never veridical, are never experiences *of* having the required two powers. I do not know of any argument for the truth of (a). It might be said that were (a) true, someone's inclination to deny its truth could be explained as produced by his conflation of an epistemic and a non-epistemic sense of 'can': he is encouraged to mistakenly suppose that he has an experience as of being able to decide to A by his half-conscious awareness that 'I can decide to A' may mean 'For all I know, I will decide to A'. But it is one thing to explain a mistake, another to show that there is a mistake to be explained. What of (b)? Certainly we often have non-veridical experiences. As dusk gathers, I may have a non-veridical experience as of the mind-independent colour of the forest changing to a darker green. But, as I am assuming, I do have veridical experiences of my own ipseical quality, and of its intensifications in my volitions. And it is hard to see why, given that much, it should not also be thought that I have veridical experiences of my power to intensify the quality.

But arguments do nevertheless suggest themselves for (b). Define Determinism (D) as the conjunction of these two theses: (i) for every instant of time, there is a proposition which expresses the state of the world at that instant; (ii) if p is a proposition which expresses the state of the world at some instant and q is a proposition that expresses the state of the world at some other instant, then the conjunction of p with the laws of nature entails q. We now have this argument:

(1) D
(2) D is incompatible with the proposition that at t N decided to A, and immediately before t had the ability to decide not to A.
(3) So N did not at t make a free decision to A.

Why (2)? Suppose that at t, N decided to A, but had the ability at t to decide not to A. Then if D is true, N had the power at t to render false the conjunction of the laws of nature and a proposition expressing the state of the world before t. But nobody has the power to render false propositions about the past. And we are equally powerless to render the laws of nature false. When (1) – (3) is supplemented by this argument for (2), we get a version of the argument for 'Incompatibilism', fully developed by Van Inwagen,[53] which has become known as the Consequence Argument.

The most obvious objection to the complete argument for (3) is that D is false or at least not known to be true. But we can construct a similar argument for the same conclusion in which D is replaced by a more restricted and perhaps more plausible doctrine linking decisions to the neurophysiological states of the decider's body. D might for example be replaced by

> D* For any true proposition p describing a decision, and any true proposition q describing the neurophysiological state just before that decision of whoever made that decision, the conjunction of q with the laws of nature entails p.

That D false or not known to be true is not, however, the only objection to the complete argument for (3). There is also the objection that some at least of the true generalisations which we call laws of nature are true only because of the way in which we exercise our powers to make decisions. And a parallel objection can be made against the revised version of the complete argument which we get when we substitute D* for D. That I decide at t to A may follow from the conjunction of a proposition about my neurophysiological state before t and a true generalisation linking decisions and neurophysiological states of the decider. But whether or not we choose to call this generalisation a law of nature, it may still be true only because I do not exercise my power to decide not to A. My neurophysiological state before t may have caused my decision to A, rather than a decision not to A, but we do not have to suppose that my neurophysiological state somehow forced or necessitated me to decide to A. We do not have to suppose that, as Ayer would have put it, an unhappy effect has tried 'vainly to escape from the clutches of an overmastering cause'.[54]

Is there an argument for (3) which does not assume that we are unable to render the laws of nature false? The following argument suggests itself.

(4) D* For any true proposition p describing a decision, and any true proposition q describing the neurophysiological state just before that decision of whoever made that decision, the conjunction of q with the laws of nature entails p
(5) N freely decided at t to A
(6) N was able at t to decide not to A (from 5)
(7) There is a true proposition describing N's neurophysiological state just before his decision to A whose conjunction with the laws of nature entails that N decided at t to A (from 4 & 5)
(8) N did not decide at t not to A (from 5)
(9) If N had decided at t not to A, his neurophysiological state just before that decision not to A would have been exactly as it was just before his actual decision to A (from 5)
(10) Whenever something like N's deciding at t not to A occurs, it is immediately preceded by a neurophysiological state exactly like N's neurophysiological state just before his actual decision to A (from (9)

34 *Human Selves*

(11) Sometimes a neurophysiological state exactly like the state that immediately preceded N's actual decision to A is immediately followed by a decision like N's decision not to A (from 10)

(12) (11) is incompatible with (7).

Since (7) follows from the conjunction of (4) and 5), it follows from (12) that (11) is incompatible with the conjunction of (4)) and (5). So, given (4), (5) is false, i.e. (3) N did not at t make a free decision to A.

Why, it will be asked, are we to infer (10) from (9)? The inference can be defended by appealing to what might be called a demystified interpretation of counterfactual conditionals. By this I mean an interpretation which takes the putting forward of a counterfactual to be nothing more than a convenient way of asserting certain propositions purely about the actual world, one at least of the propositions being a generalisation about the topics of antecedent and consequent which is indispensable in the deduction of the latter from the former. Suppose for example that you say, 'if it had been one of my books it would have had my name in it'. On a demystified interpretation of counterfactuals, this is just a convenient way of asserting that the book does not have your name in it and that all your books have your name in them. Or, to borrow an example from Quine, consider 'If Julius Caesar had been in command in Korea, he would have used the atom bomb'. On a demystified interpretation what we have here is no more than an allusion to Caesar's character, a description of the military situation in Korea, a generalisation about what commanders with that kind of character do in that kind of situation, and a reminder that Caesar was born in the wrong century. Back now to the inference of

(10) Whenever something like N's deciding at t not to A occurs, it is immediately preceded by a neurophysiological state exactly like K's neurophysiological state just before his actual decision to A.

(9) From if N had decided at t not to A, his neurophysiological state just before that decision not to A would have been exactly as it was just before his actual decision to A.

On a demystified interpretation of counterfactuals, (10) follows from (9) because (9) means no more than that N did not decide not to A and that whenever something like N's deciding at t not to A occurs, it is immediately preceded by a neurophysiological state exactly like N's neurophysiological state just before his actual decision to A.

Why, though, should we adopt a demystified interpretation of counterfactuals? Why should we not interpret counterfactuals on the lines suggested by David Lewis? On a Lewis-style interpretation 'If X had been the case, then N would have decided at t not to A' will mean something like 'Either it is impossible that X was the case, or any possible world in which X is the case and N does not decide at t not to A is less similar to the actual world than some possible world in which X is the case and N decides at t not to A'. And on a Lewis-style interpretation of counterfactuals, (10) does not follow from (9). On a Lewis-style interpretation, (9) is true if and only if either (i) it is impossible that

(A) N decides at t not to A,

or (ii) some possible world in which it is true both that (A) and that

(B) the state of the world just before t is exactly like the state of the actual world just before t

is more similar to the actual world than any world in which (A) and not-(B) both hold. But even if (10) were false, a possible world in which both (A) and (B) hold might still be more similar to the actual world than any world in which (A) and not-(B) hold. The defender of the argument (4) – (12) may try to uphold the demystified interpretation of counterfactuals in the face of the Lewis-style alternative by denying, on the basis of Empirical Atomism, that in 'possible worlds' 'possible' means anything at all.

Suppose it is agreed that D* is more plausible than D, and that we should adopt a demystified interpretation of counterfactuals which allows (10) to follow from (9). The argument for (3) is still open to the objection that even D* is either false or not known to be true. At this point it may be suggested that there is a statistical hypothesis about the natural order, more plausible than either D or D*, which is perfectly well able to replace them in an argument of the kind I gave for (3). This hypothesis is

> S For any true propositions p and q which respectively describe the world at an instant and at an earlier instant, there is a set of true spatiotemporally unrestricted statistical generalisations whose conjunction with q entails that there is a probability R ($0<R<1$) that the state of the world described by p will occur.

But now it will be objected that though S may be more plausible than either D or D*, we do not at present know of any compelling evidence either for or against the truth of any of these general hypotheses about the natural order which are to be conscripted as premises in some argument of the kind I gave for (3). There is a forceful presentation of what is in effect this objection in the final chapter of Mark Balaguer's excellent book *Free Will as an Open Scientific Problem*.[55] But so far as I can see, there is in any case no way to show, within the constraints of a demystified conception of counterfactuals, that S excludes the existence of free decisions as I define them. Suppose that the new argument for (3) which we get when D* has been replaced by S begins as follows:

(4a) S For any true propositions p and q which respectively describe the world at an instant and at an earlier instant, there is a set of true spatio-temporally unrestricted statistical generalisations whose conjunction with q entails that there is a probability R (0<R,1) that the state of the world described by p will occur.
(5) N freely decided at t to A
(6) N was able at t to decide not to A (from 5)
(7a) There is a true proposition describing N's neurophysiological state just before his decision to A whose conjunction with the laws of nature entails that there is a probability R (0<R<1) N decided at t to A (from 4a & 5)
(8) N did not decide at t not to A (from 5)
(9) If N had decided at t not to A, his neurophysiological state just before that decision not to A would have been exactly as it was just before his actual decision to A (from 5)
(10) Whenever something like N's deciding at t not to A occurs, it is immediately preceded by a neurophysiological state exactly like N's neurophysiological state just before his actual decision to A (from 9)
(11) Sometimes a neurophysiological state exactly like the state that immediately preceded N's actual decision to A is immediately followed by a decision like N's decision not to A (from 10)
(12) (11) is incompatible with (7a).

Since (12) is false, the new argument has already broken down. At this point I abandon the project of arguing against our freedom of decision by appealing to a general hypothesis about the natural order and to a demystified interpretation of counterfactuals.

With 'free decision' taken as I defined it, N freely decides to A if he decides to A straight after he has a veridical experience either as of being both able not to decide to A and in exactly the same circumstances able to decide to A, or a veridical experience as of being both able not to decide to A and in exactly the same circumstances able to decide to A. I do not of course deny that 'free decision' has or has been given other senses. On some of these, it is obvious enough that we sometimes make free decisions, and on others it is equally obvious that we never do. If you are physically forced to go through the doorway, you move through it but not of your own volition, and this movement is still in a peripheral sense an action. But a decision is always of the agent's own volition, and so is never, as a peripheral action may be, strictly speaking forced. So if by a free decision is meant an unforced decision, it is obvious enough that if we make decisions we make free decisions. But 'free decision' also has senses on which it is just as plain that free decisions are never made.

We might take it that N's decision d1 was free only if (i) he made d1 only because he had certain wants and beliefs at the time of d1, (ii) he had previously made a decision d2 to have those wants and beliefs, (iii) he made the decision d2 only because he had certain wants and beliefs at the time of d2, (iv) he had previously made a decision d3 to have those wants and beliefs, (v) he had made the decision d3 only because he had certain wants and beliefs at the time of d3, and so on ad infinitum. Here we have an infinitely regressive sense of 'free decision'. According to Galen Strawson, this infinitely regressive freedom of decision is 'the freedom that most people think matters most to them'. He thinks that only if our actions satisfy an infinitely regressive condition are we 'truly or without qualification morally responsible for our actions, responsible for them in such a way that we are 'flat-out deserving of moral praise or blame or punishment or reward for them'.[56] And that we are thus 'truly responsible' for our actions is, he thinks, a deep and widespread belief, 'central to the Western religious, moral and cultural tradition'.[57] Obviously enough, we never do make decisions which are free in this infinitely regressive sense: it is medically if not logically impossible for us to complete an infinite series of choices of principles of choice.[58] But a conjecture now suggests itself:

> (HFD) There is no single sense of 'free decision' such that both (i) there is good evidence that we never make decisions which are in this sense free, and (ii) we would on reflection *want* to make decisions which are free in this sense.

If (HFD) is true then it can at least be said that when it comes to freedom of decision, no intractable conflict afflicts us between what we want to be true and what we believe to be the case. The West need not despair! That 'free decision' has among its senses the one that I defined in terms of a dual power does not falsify (HFD) because there seems not to be any good evidence that we never make decisions in this sense free. Is (HFD) falsified by the existence of the infinitely regressive sense of 'free decision' that Strawson equates with 'morally responsible decision'? There is a simple reason to doubt that (HFD) is falsified by the existence of Strawson's infinitely regressive sense. It is that our very realisation that it is impossible for us to make decisions in this sense free will in the end destroy any desire we may have to make them. According to Hume, 'Nothing is more certain than that despair has almost the same effect upon us with enjoyment, and that we are no sooner acquainted with the impossibility of satisfying any desire, than the desire itself vanishes'.[59] That is of course false. But one might well think that a want does not forever survive its owner's conviction that it is impossible to satisfy. Suppose there is a time at which you want both now to have your cake and now to eat it. One might well think that you cannot forever sustain this want in full awareness that it has an incoherent content.

But there is also a more subtle reason for denying that the existence of Strawson's infinitely regressive sense falsifies (HFD).

It is that 'free decision' has a further sense on which it is perfectly possible to make free decisions, and which bears a close enough resemblance to Strawson's infinitely regressive sense for it to be plausible to suppose that you would regard decisions free in this sense as to all intents and purposes just as good as decisions free in Strawson's infinitely regressive sense. The realisation that this substitute is available will dispel any desire you may have to be free in Strawson's sense. You are free in this further sense (I will call it the SA sense) if and only if (1) you had a reason R1 for which you made it, (2) either you decided to bring about in yourself, or you decided to leave alone, at least one of the mental states constitutive of your having R1, and you had a reason R2 for that R1-related decision, (3) either you decided to bring about in yourself, or you decided to leave alone, at least one of the mental states constitutive of your having R2, and you had a reason R3 for that R2-related decision, and so on, ad infinitum. The mental states constitutive of having a reason for a decision are, as I take it, wants and beliefs: you have a reason for a decision if you want something to which, as you believe, the decision is conducive. To simplify matters, let me initially suppose that it is a sufficient condition for you to make an SA-free decision that you had a reason R1 for which you made the decision and you decided to leave as it was the want element in your having R1, and you had a reason R2 for making the decision to leave the R1-related want element as it was, and you made the decision to leave the R2- related want element as it was, and so on ad infinitum. You cannot take a decision free in Strawson's sense without having taken an infinite number of other decisions. But there is no such difficulty about taking an SA-free decision. To see this, suppose that your reason R1 for making a decision d1 was that you wanted G and believed that d1 was conducive to G. Now suppose that you decided to leave as it was your want for G, and that you had a reason R2 for making that last decision. This reason R2 may perfectly well have been just that your deciding to leave your desire for G alone <u>was conducive to G itself</u>. And in this case the want element in your having R2 will again be your want for G. Next suppose that you decided to leave as it was the want element in your having R2. This want element, it has emerged, is a want for G. But in this case you will have decided to leave as it was the want element in your having R2 <u>without having made any decision distinct from your decision to leave it was the want element in your having R1</u>. If your making the decision was SA-free responsible, you will of course have made a decision to leave as it was the want element in your having a reason R3 for deciding leaving as it was the want element in your having R2. But if the want element in your having R3 was just a want for G, and your reason for deciding to leaving as it was your want for G was that your having it was conducive to G itself, then your reason for deciding to leaving as it was the want element in your having R3 will again have been that wanting G was conducive to G itself. The want element in your having R3 will accordingly also be a want for G itself, and you will have decided to leave that want element alone again without having made any decision distinct from your decision to leave as it was want element in your having R1. And so on, ad infinitum. Your decision d1 can thus satisfy the sufficient condition I gave for its being SA-free without your having made any decision to leave a want as it was which was distinct from your decision to leave as it was the want element in your having R1. And so your decision d1 can have been SA-free without your having made an infinite number of distinct decisions.

There is of course certain artificiality about my case of someone making an SA-free decision without having made an infinite number of distinct decisions. Why after all should you make a decision just because you think it conducive to a single desideratum G? Surely you will have other desiderata which you will also want to take into account. Similarly, if you are wondering whether to leave as it is your desire for G, you may indeed consider the effects of your continuing to want G on G itself, but will you not also want to consider its effects on the other things you want? Perhaps this extra realism can be accommodated. Suppose that R1 is that the decision d1 is somehow conducive to the whole aggregate of things you want. The want element in your having R1 will then be a whole aggregate of wanting. You may perfectly well decide to leave this whole aggregate alone on the grounds that this decision is somehow conducive to the whole corresponding aggregate of things wanted.

Could you make an SA-free decision without having made an infinite number of decisions if to be SA-responsible you had to take decisions not just about the want elements of your reasons but also about their belief elements? Suppose you had a reason R1 for which you made the decision d1, and R1 was that you wanted G and believed that d1 was conducive to G. If your decision d1 was SA-free in a belief-including way, then either you will have decided to bring about the belief element in your having R1 or, finding that you already had this belief, you will have decided to leave it as it was. Suppose you deliberately left the belief as it was. Then you will have had a reason R2 for doing that, if your decision d1 was SA-free. Surely the belief element in your having R2 will be different from the belief element in your having R1 and vicious infinite regression will accordingly ensue? I can provide the beginnings of an answer. Suppose you believe that p, and that your reason for continuing to believe that p is composed of a desire to believe the truth and of a belief that p is true. The belief element in your having a reason to continue to believe that p will not then pose a practical problem which is distinct from the problem of whether to continue to believe that p. For if you have a reason for continuing to believe that p, then ipso facto you have a reason for continuing to believe that p is true. And if, as we are assuming, you do indeed believe that p, nothing is more likely than that you also believe that p is true. If, wanting to believe the truth, you ask yourself whether, if you continue to believe that p, you will believe the truth, and then the mere fact that you do already believe that p will set your mind at rest.

1.9 Ulterior?

A transcendent self is one that causes both the existence of any non-abstract nonselves there may be which are not composed of selves, and the existence of all those selves which do not cause the existence of every other self. Ulterior selves I define as selves which are constituents of material objects, and a material object I define as a concrete and substantial nonself, no component of which is a transcendent self, and events in which cause experiences as of what commonsense takes to be material objects, experiences, for example, as of brains, or arms and legs, or stones and trees. A group of selves is not a self, but it may nevertheless have the independence necessary for it to be a substance. And a substantial nonself may be composed of non-transcendent selves. I end this chapter with a word on the hypothesis that our own selves are ulterior, and, more particularly, that they are constituents of the material objects events in which cause our experiences as of human brains. It is a hypothesis whose conjunction with the hypothesis that selves are indestructible has the striking consequence that what commonsense takes to be the final decay and disintegration of a human brain may be no more than an appearance caused by some radical re-alignment of the selves which, composing a material object, earlier caused the appearance of an intact human brain.

You may be reminded of a hypothesis about mind and matter which was proposed by the later Bertrand Russell, after he had moved away from neutral monism. Russell proposed that the events making up a living brain are actually identical with those which make up the corresponding mind. Against materialist psycho-physical identity theories, Russell insisted that mental events are not topic-neutral inner events of which we know nothing except that they are apt to cause overt behaviour, but rather events with whose intrinsic qualities we are perfectly well acquainted by introspection: it is the non-causal properties of matter about which we are entirely ignorant, or at least the non-causal properties of any matter which does not compose a living human brain. 'When we come to events in physical space time where there are no brains ..., the qualities of such events are unknown-so completely unknown that we cannot say either that they are, or that they are not, different from the qualities that we know as belonging to mental events'.[60] For Russell, we know nothing of extra-cerebral matter except what we can infer by means of certain abstract postulates about the purely logical attributes of its space-time distribution. But there are obvious differences between Russell's hypothesis and the hypothesis that I am now considering about the ulteriority of human selves. One difference is that with 'ulterior' taken as I define it, a self is ulterior only if it is a constituent of a material object which is a *substantial* nonself, whereas Russell denied the existence of substances of any kind. For Russell, the mind is series of events which is both mental and material, rather than a substance in the sense of an enduring and independent object with changing states. The 'substance-philosophy' is, he thought, a superstition 'evolved by the original metaphysicians who invented language, who were much struck by the difference between their enemy in battle and their enemy after he had been slain, although they were persuaded that it was the same person whom they first feared, and then ate'.[61]

I seem however to detect a difficulty in the hypothesis that our selves are ulterior by virtue of composing the material objects events in which cause our experiences as of our brains. The difficulty is that it does not seem possible to square the hypothesis with doctrine that our selves are in at least some phases of their existence embodied. On the definition that I gave in section 1.5, a self is embodied only if there is a body events in which are directly causally related to mental events which belong to that self. But on Humean principles, a mental event cannot cause or be caused by an event in a self on which that mental event depends. So a mental event cannot cause or be caused by an event in a body if that bodily event is identical to an event in a self on which that mental event depends. But how, if this self is a constituent of a material object events in which cause experiences as of a brain, can events in that self *not* be identical to events in the body to which mental events belonging to that self are supposed to be causally related?

Notes

1. See Crane (2001), 32–3.
2. Why 'as of' rather than 'of'? To say that you have an experience of an x is in my usage to imply that the x is real and the experience veridical. To say that you have an experience as of an x is leave open the question of whether the x is real and the experience veridical.
3. Zahavi and Kriegel (2015), 36.
4. Ibid., 36.
5. Zahavi (2011), 59.
6. Hume (1978), *Treatise*, Book 1, sect. 6.
7. Hopkins (1959), *Sermons and Devotional Writings*, 123.
8. Galen Strawson insists that it is perfectly possible for there to be an awareness on the part of the subject of experience of itself as it is in the present moment of experience. He thinks that this awareness is the same as 'awareness or consciousness of the awareness or consciousness that it itself is', an awareness of awareness as to whose reality there is, among mediators, 'an extremely robust consensus' (2009a), 180. But if the subject of experience *is* an awareness or consciousness, and if a consciousness is an experience, then how can it be that, as Strawson also thinks, it is impossible for an experience to exist 'without the polarity of experience and experiential content' [(2009a), 274]?
9. Robinson (2007), 57.

42 *Human Selves*

10 Hume, *Treatise*, 252. Cf. Swinburne (1997), 177: '…there seems to me nothing contradictory in allowing to a substance many beginnings of existence'. More recently, Swinburne has defended the doctrine that humans have 'a vast number of largely unconscious categorical mental states, beliefs, and desires connected to each other in rational ways' (2013), 166–69. Here, 'unconscious mental state' means mental states of which its owner is not conscious. On this doctrine, there is no temptation to suppose that sometimes we stop existing and then start again.
11 Ginet, in his excellent book *On Action*, calls it an 'actish phenomenal quality', and thinks that, at least in the case of bodily action, it is always experienced though not always noticed [Ginet, (1990), 25].
12 Broad (1952), 215.
13 *Philosophical Commentaries*, 829. Cf. Lloyd (1985).
14 For an exhaustive exploration of Kant's idea, see Longuenesse (2017).
15 Stein (2006), 425.
16 Hopkins (1959), *Sermons and Devotional Writings*, 123.
17 The Dissimilarity of the Diverse is what McTaggart called the principle, and his name is better because the Identity of Indiscernibles 'misleadingly suggests that there are indiscernibles, in the plural, but these stand in an identity-relation' [Geach (1979), 47].
18 Black (1952), 153–64.
19 ibid., 33.
20 Swinburne (1997), 341. That a substance has thisness does not mean that it has an individual essence, where a 'property or set of properties φ is an individual essence of an object A if A has φ essentially, and no other actual or possible object has φ' [Mackie (2006), 19]. The idea has been mooted that t if A has the property of being identical to A, then this property is not simply relational. 'It may be more appropriate to think of it as being a special kind of intrinsic property…We might think of each object as having a special and necessarily unshareable intrinsic property of being the very thing that it is… For historical reasons, such a property is called a *haecceity*' [Lowe (2002), 102]. That a substance has thisness does not mean that it has a haecceity.
21 Broad (1962), 430.
22 Dainton (2016), 7. As one may have experiences as of a scarlet poppy, so, I grant, one may have experiences as of a something behind one's eyes and between one's ears. But I rather doubt that one has experiences as of a something a couple of inches behind one's eyes and between one's ears having an experience as of a scarlet poppy. Here the content seems too complex for all its elements to be so definite. If I have an experience as of a something having an experience as of a scarlet poppy, it is too much to expect both the 'as of a scarlet poppy' part to be definite, and the something to have a definite location in a phenomenal space.
23 Foster (2008), vii.
24 Cf. Hasker (2001), 122–44. I will not try to show that what now follows is quite the same as anything that Hasker says.
25 Bayne (2010), 217.
26 Goetz (2018), 310.
27 See Wiggins (1995), Simons (1998) and Broackes (2006).
28 Williams (1966), ch. 7.
29 Williams (1966), 89.
30 Lewis (1989).
31 Foster (1985), 34.
32 Ibid., 35.

33 Ibid., 36.
34 Ibid., 36.
35 Cf. Olson (2001), 81.
36 Dainton (2010), 303.
37 Dainton (2010), 303.
38 Strawson (2009a), 12.
39 Strawson (2017a), 97.
40 'Ontic structural realism' is the standard label for the kind of scientific realism which says that the explanatory entities are just relations. 'Epistemic structural realists' say that of the properties which scientific theories attribute to the explanatory entities, it is only the relational properties that we know or should believe that they really have. See Ladyman and Ross (2007), ch. 3.
41 That is attempted in Bayne (2010).
42 See section 1.4 above.
43 Papineau (2009), 57.
44 Papineau (2009), 59.
45 Körner (1966), 221.
46 Körner (1966), 229.
47 Kim (2018), 161.
48 Kim (2018), 161.
49 Foster (1991), 163.
50 For a useful discussion of some of these drawbacks and advantages, see Hong Yu Wong (2007), 181–93.
51 Foster (1991), 166. He also doubts whether the possibility would be all that remote 'in the case of two monozygotic twins with very brief, e.g., entirely pre-natal, lives' (166). (i)–(iii) is evidence that this too is no more than a possibility.
52 Frankfurt (1969), 828–39.
53 Van Inwagen (1983).
54 Ayer (1959), 283.
55 Balaguer (2010).
56 Strawson (2002), 457.
57 Strawson (1994), 8.
58 Strawson thinks that there are situations in which experience makes it impossible not to believe that one is making a 'truly responsible' decision. If that is true, then just for the sake of not being under an illusion, one might well on reflection want it to be true that in these practical situations one really does make infinitely regressive decisions. What practical situations does he have in mind? 'You set off for a shop on the evening of a national holiday, intending to buy a cake with your last ten pound note. On the steps of the shop someone is shaking an Oxfam tin. You stop, and it seems completely clear to you that it is entirely up to you what you do next. That is, it seems to you that you are truly, radically free to choose, in such a way that you will be ultimately responsible for whatever you do choose' [Strawson (1994), 10]. Strawson admits that there are further questions to be asked about 'why human beings experience these situations of choice as they do. 'It is an interesting question whether any cognitively sophisticated, rational, self-conscious agents must experience situations of choice in this way. But they are the experiential rock on which the belief in true moral responsibility is founded' [(1994), 10–11]. This strikes me as quite implausible. Anything can be believed. But there are limits to what can be experienced. That one has already taken an infinite number of distinct decisions falls outside the limits of experience. And even if there were such an experience of the infinite, why, independently of our

desire not to be deluded, would we want all our decisions to be made because of the way we were, 'mentally speaking' at the time? Why would we not be happy enough sometimes to make decisions which have no such mental causes? Strawson does consider the thought that one's decisions are taken by an 'agent-self' which is 'in some crucial way independent of one's general mental nature N, one's overall character, personality, motivational structure'. But, he asks, what happens 'when one faces a difficult choice between X, doing one's duty, and Y, following one's non-moral desires? Well, given N, one responds in a certain way. One is swayed by reasons for and against both X and Y. One tends towards X or Y, given N. But one is an agent-self independent of N, and one can be [morally responsible for what one does] in a situation like this even if (even though) one cannot be morally responsible for N, because although...N certainly *inclines* one to do one thing rather than another, it does not thereby *necessitate* one to do one thing rather than the other....That, at least, is the story. The agent self decides in the light of N but is not determined by N and is therefore free. But the following question arises: *Why* does the agent self decide as it does? And the general answer is clear. Whatever the agent-self decides, it decides as it does because of the overall way it is; it too must have a nature - call it N*- of some sort. And this necessary truth returns us to where we started. Once again it seems that the agent-self must be responsible for N*. But this is impossible [for that would require it already to have made an infinite number of decisions]' [Strawson (2002), 457]. Why, though, must there be *any* answer to the question of why the agent self decides as it does? Why should it be so distressing to suppose that the agent-self makes some inexplicable decisions?

59 *Treatise*, xviii.
60 Russell (1948), 246–7.
61 Russell (1956), 143.

2 ULTERIOR SELVES?

A transcendent self is one that causes both the existence of any non-abstract nonselves there may be which are not composed of selves, and the existence of all those selves which do not cause the existence of every other self. Ulterior selves I define as selves which are constituents of material objects, and material objects I define as concrete and substantial nonselves, of which no constituent is a transcendent self, and events in which cause experiences as of what common sense takes to be material objects, experiences, for example, as of brains, or arms and legs, or stones and trees. A group of selves is not a self, but it may nevertheless have the independence necessary for it to be a substance. Material objects, as I have just defined them, could be substantial nonselves with ulterior selves as their constituents. I rejected the quasi-Russelian doctrine that our own selves compose the material objects which cause the experiences we enjoy as of human brains. I will now assume that our own selves are in no other way ulterior. But that is an assumption which is perfectly compatible with the thesis that at least some material objects are composed of selves analogous to ours, are composed of selves which like ours are disseveralities, but whose ipseical qualities are no more than akin to those qualities of ours which memory can reveal. Are there such ulterior selves?

Suppose that

(HS) Every substance is either a self or composed of selves.

Then if, as I have defined them, there are material objects, they are composed of selves, and so ulterior selves exist. HS is of course compatible with Berkeleyan Idealism, which denies that there are ulterior selves. But for the Berkeleyan Idealist, there are no material objects for ulterior selves to compose. A material object is a substantial nonself, of which no constituent is a transcendent self, and events in which cause our experiences as of, for example, stones and tree. But for the Berkeleyan Idealist, only God causes such experiences. Taking for granted that there are material objects, I shall in this chapter consider arguments for the truth of HS.

DOI: 10.4324/9781003274483-3

Why yet another acronym? Might not 'Panpsychism' be a better label for the doctrine that I am calling HS? The difficulty is that there are some other rather different doctrines to which the label 'Panpsychism' has already been affixed. Galen Strawson writes that 'Pure panpsychism is the view that the intrinsic nature - the stuff - of all concrete reality is consciousness, live, occurrent, conscious experience, experiential "what-its-likeness", *experientiality* or *experience* for short'. 'Every substance is either a self or composed of selves'; it does not however entail that all reality is consciousness. For a self, as I define selfhood, can exist without being conscious. Philip Goff writes that 'Panpsychism as it is defended in contemporary science and philosophy is the view that *consciousness is fundamental and ubiquitous*'.[1] Since only substances are fundamental, and selves are substances which can exist without being conscious, 'consciousness is fundamental' is actually incompatible with the doctrine that every substance is either a self or composed of selves. *Ipseicism* will be my new chosen label for doctrine that I called HS.

The most obvious way to argue for Ipseicism is to claim that every substance must have an intrinsic property, such as a colour, as well as a causal or structural or dispositional property of the kind attributed to it by science, that the only available intrinsic property is a property of consciousness, that there can be no consciousness without a subject, and that this subject must be a self. Of the three arguments for Ipseicism now to be considered, the third bears a certain resemblance to this piece of reasoning. The other two arguments are quite different.

One invokes the principle that in nature there are no radical discontinuities. The other invokes our ignorance. You could perhaps argue for the existence of ulterior selves without first arguing for Ipseicism. I suspect, however, that no such independent argument is available which does not appeal to the implications of what an ostensibly revealed religion teaches about the destiny of human bodies, or about our present relationship to the body of a transcendent self. And no case is here made for the truth of any ostensibly revealed religion.

2.1 Continuity

The first argument for Ipseicism that I want to consider is about continuity. It goes as follows.

(1) In nature there are no radical discontinuities
(2) There was a time before which there were no human selves
(3) The causes of the emergence of the first human self or selves were events in substances
(4) These substances were or were composed of selves (from 1, 2, 3)
(5) Every substance is either a self or composed of selves (from 1, 4)

How are we supposed to get (4) from (1), (2) and (3)? The thought is that if the causes of the emergence of the first human self or selves had been anything other than events in substances which were selves or groups of selves, then nature would have been radically discontinuous, which (1) says that it is not. How are we supposed to get to (5) from (1) and (4)? The thought is that given (1) there will be continuity not just between the first human self or selves and the substances out of which they are supposed to have emerged, but between those ancestral substances and all other substances.

Why should we believe that in nature there are no radical discontinuities? There are philosophers who are happy to treat that principle or some principle very like it as an axiom. So, for example, in the case he makes for the doctrine that 'everything is experiential', Galen Strawson assumes without argument 'the old metaphysical thesis ... *natura non facit saltum*, i.e.(roughly) there are no absolute or radical discontinuities in nature'.[2] Something similar seems also to have been assumed in well-known arguments once mounted against substance Dualism and in favour of a Materialist Theory of the Mind. Witness Armstrong:

> It seems that the Dualist must conceive of the emergence of mind in the following way. At some time after conception, when the nervous system of man and the higher animals reaches a certain degree of complexity, a completely new non-spatial entity is brought into existence in a completely new sort of relation to the body. The emergence of this new entity could not have been predicted from laws that deal with the physical properties of physical things. Already the account is highly implausible from the scientific point of view. It is not a particularly difficult notion that, when the nervous system reaches a certain level of complexity, it should develop new properties. Nor would there be anything particularly difficult in the notion that when the nervous system reaches a certain level of complexity it should affect something that was already in existence in a new way. But it is quite a different matter to hold that the central nervous system should have the power to create something else, of a quite different nature from itself, and create it out of new materials.[3]

Anxious to preserve continuity between human selves and the substances events in which first caused them to emerge, some philosophers have hoped to show that though seemingly simple, human selves are nevertheless, like pre-human substances, composed of myriads of simple selves. They have struggled then to show how these myriads can combine into single human selves, to solve what has become known in Panpsychist circles as the Combination Problem.[4] Accepting the insolubility of the Combination Problem, at least one writer has sought to uphold nature's radical continuity by postulating a continuity between human selves and a cosmic self

48 *Ulterior Selves?*

which grounds them in the sense that they are all mere aspects of it.[5] But for present purposes I do not need to explore this speculation. To question the argument (1) – (5), it is enough just to question the doctrine that in nature there are no radical discontinuities. I argue in Chapter 3 for the existence of at least one transcendent self which causes the existence of all human selves. If that argument is sound, then the first human selves were caused to exist not by pre-human substances composed of myriads of simple selves but rather by something radically discontinuous with the rest of what exists.

2.2 Ignorance and Simplicity

The next argument for Ipseicism that I want to consider is quite naïve. It goes as follows.

(6) We know that there are selves
(7) Ipseicism is a simpler hypothesis than the hypothesis that some substances are selves or groups of selves and some are neither
(8) We do not know that Ipseicism is false
(9) So (9) Probably Ipseicism is true

In its structure, (6) – (9) resembles a pan-experientialist argument proposed by Galen Strawson, namely

(6a) We know that the 'human experiential' exists
(7a) That everything is experiential is 'a more parsimonious hypothesis about the nature of physical reality' than that some things are experiential and some are not
(8a) 'There isn't a scintilla of a reason for postulating anything nonexperiential'
(9a) So (9a) Probably everything is experiential[6]

How are we supposed to reach (9) from (6) – (8)? By an inference to the best explanation? Is the thought that the conjunction of (6) and (8) is more simply explained by Ipseicism than by its negation? The objection would then be that whether or not Ipseicism is true, it is not too difficult to explain the truth of (6) and (8). The explanation could be just that although our cognitive capacities are sufficient for us to know that there are selves, they are insufficient for us to know that there are substances which are neither selves nor groups of selves. We have experiences as of stones and trees, and take it that these experiences are caused by substances, and for all we know these substances are groups of selves. But it is not as if, after observing many and various entities, we find that some are substances which are either selves or groups of selves, and though we might have found that some are neither this we never do. Even if some substances are neither selves nor groups of selves, this is not something that mere observation can be expected to tell us. And, anyway, if there are any entities that we know to be selves, they are just our own selves and those of other people. Such selves are many and various, but the variety may not stretch to encompass the rather different kinds of selves which might compose material objects. There are analogous difficulties with (6a) – (9a). How do we know that though we have no reason to suppose that there is 'anything nonexperiential', this does not just reveal a limit to our powers of reason? Might not the 'human experiential' which we do know to exist be quite different from the experiential which according to (9a) makes up everything else?

There is an inviting simplicity in monistic doctrines like Ipseicism, and monists of one kind or another have often advanced arguments analogous to (6) – (9). Attempts were once made to derive Materialism from the premises 'we know that some states are material', '"all states are material" is a simpler hypothesis than "some states are material and some are not"', and 'we do not know of any state that it is not material'. It was by similar reasoning that Schopenhauer concluded that the world is Will. 'Spinoza (ep.62) says that if a stone flying through the air had consciousness, it would imagine that it was flying of its own will. I add merely that the stone would be right...what in the case of the stone appears as cohesion, gravitation, rigidity in the assumed condition is by its inner nature the same as what I recognise in myself as will, and which the stone would recognise as will, if knowledge were added in its case also'.[7] The monistic conclusions of such arguments are to some people powerfully attractive. What, though, are the credentials of the principle of inference which these arguments employ?

2.3 The Confinement of Qualities

I turn finally to a more complex argument for Ipseicism. It derives in part from McTaggart's *Nature of Existence*, and aims to reduce Ipseicism's negation to absurdity. It relies on the principle that every substance has a sufficient description, in the sense of a description which applies only to that substance, and which does not mention any other substance: a sufficient description is couched in entirely general terms. The argument is this.

(10) There is a substance x which is neither a self nor composed of selves (supposition for reductio)
(11) Every substance has a sufficient description
(12) x has a sufficient description (from 10 and 11)
(13) Every entity with a sufficient description is either a self or is composed of selves or is dependent on at least one self.
(14) x is either a self or is composed of selves or is dependent on a self (from 12 and 13)
(15) No entity dependent on a self is a substance
(16) x is either a self or composed of selves (from 14 and 15)

Why suppose that every substance has a sufficient description? Here is McTaggart's answer. By the principle of the Dissimilarity of the Diverse, no two substances have the same qualities. So every substance has an exclusive description, which is to say a description which applies only to it. Suppose that substance A1 has no sufficient description. Then any exclusive description of A1 must describe it by a relation in which it stands to a certain other substance A2. And this other substance A2 must itself have no sufficient description. For, if A2 did have a sufficient description D, then A1 could be sufficiently described as the particular which has this relation to the only instance of D. Now A2 will have an exclusive description. And since this cannot be a sufficient description, A2 must be exclusively described by a certain relation in which it stands to a certain other substance A3. But if A1 has no sufficient description, then again A3 cannot have a sufficient description. So if by the Dissimilarity of the Diverse every substance has an exclusive description, and if A1 has no sufficient description, there is an infinite series of substances A1, A2, A3, ...the exclusive description of each member of which is wholly dependent on the description of its successor. And this is absurd.[8]

(11) is one needy premise in the would-be reductio (10) – (16). But there is another needy premise, namely

(13) Every entity with a sufficient description is either a self or is composed of selves or is dependent on at least one self

What can be said for (13)? If an entity has a sufficient description, then it has a property whose description does not mention any particular substance and is couched in entirely general terms. Such are the ipseical qualities of selves, and likewise such sensory qualities as those of taste, smell, warmth and colour. Assume for the moment that the only completely general properties are sensory qualities and the ipseical qualities of selves. Call a quality unconfined if it is possessed by some entity other than a self or an entity dependent on a self. It may seem that of sensory qualities the only ones which it is even meaningful to count as unconfined are colour qualities. Intentional contents depend on selves. So if it can be shown that colour qualities are confined to intentional contents, then we have an argument for (13). The only completely general properties left to figure in sufficient descriptions will be the ipseical qualities of selves and the sensory qualities of their dependents. And since, as (15) says, the dependent of a substance is not a substance, (16) is within easy reach.

But can it be shown that colour qualities are confined to intentional contents? I doubt it, and suggest that for all we know colour qualities are possessed by substantial nonselves. Is there then some sound argument for (13) which does not have as a premise that colour qualities are confined to

Ulterior Selves? 51

intentional contents? Not that I know of. So (13) is doubtful, and so therefore likewise is the whole argument (10)–(16).

Why exactly is it supposed to be so sure that colour qualities are not possessed by substantial nonselves? That substantial nonselves have colour qualities does not entail that there is a substantial nonself, and a particular colour quality, such that we know that this colour quality is possessed by that nonself. It does not entail that there is any substantial nonself which we can perceive to have a particular colour quality. That substantial nonselves have colour qualities does not entail that there is any regular correlation between our experiences as of things with particular colour qualities, and the actual colour qualities that they possess. That when you have an experience as of a scarlet poppy, the poppy has some colour quality does not entail that it has a scarlet colour. For all you know, its particular colour quality may be bright blue. But equally, that you do not know that its colour quality is not bright blue does not entail that it has no colour quality at all. Let Colour Primitivism is to be our name for the doctrine that substantial nonselves have colour qualities. Colour Primitivism does not entail that we ever perceive a particular substantial nonself to have a particular colour quality. To establish Ipseicism by means of the argument (10)–(16), we must refute Colour Primitivism. But it is not necessary for us to show that we know, of any substantial nonself, just what particular colour quality it has.

Against Colour Primitivism, I know of just four things that have been or could be said. The first is that an analogy shows Colour Primitivism to be dubiously 'coherent'. John McDowell says that he would 'sympathise' with anyone who believed in the incoherence of 'a conception of amusingness which was fully intelligible otherwise than in terms of the characteristic human responses to what is amusing, but which nevertheless contrived somehow to maintain the "phenomenal" aspect of amusingness as we experience it in those responses', and he would in the same way sympathise with someone who finds it incoherent to suppose that there are colours 'which characterise things independently of their perceivers' and yet resemble colours as they figure in our experience.[9] McDowell's sympathy seems to me misplaced. Consider the sentence 'There is a scarlet poppy in the field', with 'scarlet' here taken as the name of a quality. It is sufficient for this sentence to be meaningful that, on the same interpretation of 'scarlet', the sentence 'I am having an experience as of a scarlet poppy in the flower-bed' is meaningful. And the latter sentence is indeed meaningful. We do have such experiences, and it is because we have such experiences that we form such pre-reflective beliefs as that there are intrinsically scarlet poppies in flower-beds. These pre-reflective beliefs may be false, and the experiences on which they are based may be non-veridical. But we do have experiences as of mind-independent and non-dispositionally scarlet poppies, and descriptions of the contents of these experiences have meanings. While we do have experiences, veridical or otherwise, as of coloured things which do

52 Ulterior Selves?

not depend on us, we have no such experiences as of things which do not depend on us but are 'phenomenally' amusing. It is this difference which makes McDowell's sympathy appropriate in the case of the person who denies the coherence of the amusingness conception, but inappropriate in the case of the person who denies the coherence of the colour conception.

A second objection to Colour Primitivism that there is nothing that it explains. Grant for the moment that

> (P1) If q is a set of experiential data, then q is good evidence for p if and only if p is entailed by the best explanation of q.

And grant that if (P1) is true, then there is no good evidence for the contingent truth of Colour Primitivism. It does not follow that if (P1) is true, then there is good evidence for the falsity of that hypothesis. There might of course be good evidence for its falsity if it were true that

> (P2) The explanatory redundancy of a proposition not entailed by experiential data is good evidence for the falsity of that proposition.

But why should we accept (P2)? There are philosophers who accept some such principle on grounds of parsimony. Jackson maintains in Chapter 8 of his *Perception* that 'we have no reason to believe that material things are coloured', and from here he moves to the conclusion that it is 'reasonable to assert that...colour...is not a property of material things'. He says that 'although the precise status of Ockham's razor is a matter of dispute, it seems clear that properties we have no reason to believe are possessed by material things are properties we ought not to ascribe to them'.[10] Mackie makes a similar move in his *Problems from Locke*: '...the literal ascription of colours, as we see colours, and the like, to material things, to light, and so on, forms no part of the explanation of what goes on in the physical world in the processes which lead on to our having the sensations and perceptions that we have...admittedly physics does not itself tell us that no such properties are there. This denial is a further, philosophical step; but it is one which is at least prima facie reasonable in the light of the successes of physical theory'.[11] 'The philosophical principle of economy of postulation...supplies a reason for not introducing supposedly objective qualities of kinds for which physics has no need'.[12] I should have thought, however, that it is in a way less parsimonious to believe a proposition false than merely to believe that there is no evidence for its truth.

Next, a famous thought of Russell's.

> There is no colour which pre-eminently appears to be *the* colour of the table, or even of any one particular part of the table - it appears to be of different colours from different points of view... And...Even from a given point of view the colour will seem different by artificial light, or

to a colour-blind man, or to a man wearing blue spectacles, while in the dark there will be no colour at all, though to touch and hearing the table will be unchanged. Thus colour is not something inherent in the table, but something depending upon the table and the spectator and the way the light falls on the table. When, in ordinary life, we speak of the colour of the table, we only mean the sort of colour which it will seem to have to a normal spectator from an ordinary point of view under usual conditions of light. But the other colours which appear under other conditions have just as good a right to be considered real; and therefore, to avoid favouritism, we are compelled to deny that, in itself, the table has any one particular colour.[13]

Russell thinks that if, for each particular colour quality which the table appears to have, we lack good evidence that it has that quality, then it would be favouritism to believe that it has any colour quality at all. Suppose that it is indeed favouritism to believe that p when there is no better evidence for p than there is for not-p. Then for all that Russell's reasoning shows, it is favouritism to believe, with Russell, that the table has no colour quality. For all his reasoning shows, there is no better evidence for that hypothesis than there is for the hypothesis that it has some intrinsic colour property or other, we know not which.

Lastly, an argument against Colour Primitivism which invokes the principle of the Infinite Partition of Extended Substances (IP). IP says that every extended substance has parts, which again have parts, and so on to infinity. Given IP, it could be argued that if substantial nonselves are extended substances with colour qualities, then every substantial nonself has an infinite number of parts each with a different colour. And then it could be argued that this consequence is precluded by the finitude of the range of colours. There will be too few colours to go round. Why so? Because (a) only a finite number of colours are distinguishable by conscious beings; and (b) there is no sense in the idea of a colour which no conscious being can be aware of.

(a) seems quite easy to accept. Human beings can distinguish around ten million colours, and maybe other conscious beings can distinguish vastly more. But surely there is no reason to think that for any finite number, however large, some conscious being can distinguish more than that number of colours.

(b) needs rather more support. If a quality which no being can be aware of is a colour quality, then it must share with the colours we are aware of that common feature which makes the colours we are aware of colours rather than qualities of some other kind. But there does not seem to be any such feature common to the qualities we are aware of other than a feature which in fact entails that these colours can be experienced. And so a quality, which no being can be aware of, cannot share this common feature. What then is it that makes the colours we are aware of all colours? Perhaps it is nothing more than that the experience of any two of them generates the conviction that they have some distinguishing feature in common. According to Schopenhauer, the only genuinely common feature of Hegel's dialectical transitions is that each is more tiresome than its predecessor. The unity of colour might have an analogous subjectivity. It is consistent with this account of what makes a quality a colour that you can experience a colour that I cannot. Your experience-generated conviction that quality X has something in common with blue and with red, and with yellow, can be of the same kind as my more limited experience-generated conviction that blue has something in common with red and with yellow.

But if this last argument against Colour Primitivism is to convince, a case must be supplied for the Infinite Partition principle. McTaggart believed that a more general Infinite Partition principle was self evident and ultimate, namely the doctrine that 'every substance has parts, which again have other parts, and so on to infinity'.[14] He thought that this is self-evident because it does not need proof, and that it is ultimate because it cannot be proved from any proposition more clearly self-evident.[15] And on the conjunction of this unrestricted Infinite Partition principle and the principle that every substance has a sufficient description, McTaggart built a spectacularly ingenious argument for the conclusion that every substance either is or belongs to a group of selves, each member of which is continuously perceiving both itself and every other member. Were that conclusion true, there would be no substantial nonselves with colour qualities. And the reasoning would moreover be wrecked on which, in section 1.5, I based the doctrine that simultaneously existing selves are to be distinguished from each other by their different ipseical qualities. For in that reasoning I appealed to the existence of simultaneously existing unconscious selves.[16] But I am no more able to make a case for the general Infinite Partition principle than I am for the restricted principle which applies only to extended substances.

The argument (10) – (16) tries to reduce Ipseicism's negation to absurdity. But the argument does not work unless we know that Colour Primitivism is false. We have no such knowledge. So the argument does not work.[17]

Notes

1 Goff (2017b), 107
2 Strawson (2017b), 82
3 Armstrong (1968), 30
4 See Chalmers (2017)
5 See Goff (2017a), chs 8–9
6 Strawson (2017a), 101–2. We might think that (6a) – (9a) is not just analogous to (7) – (9) but can be developed into an argument for the same conclusion. Might we not say since there can be no experience without a subject of that experience, and since this subject can only be a self, Ipseicism can

be derived from 'Everything is experiential'? We might indeed say this. But Strawson would demur. For Strawson, a subject of experience is not a self as I have defined selfhood, but a 'sesmet', a fleeting conscious subject which lasts no longer than a 'lived-present-of-experience', i.e., 'for no more than half a second' [Strawson (2009a), 252].

7 *The World as Will and Representation*, I, 126. Cf. Max Scheler on the German bombardment of Rheims cathedral in the First World War: 'if the cathedral had been capable of thinking and feeling it would have realized that the force firing the cannon was part of the same force that had once created this heaven-storming Gothic masterpiece' [quoted in Grunberger (1974), 386–7].
8 See McTaggart (1921), 104–9
9 McDowell (1983), 4
10 Jackson (1977), 123
11 Mackie (1976), 18–19
12 Mackie (1976), 20
13 Russell (1912), 13–14
14 McTaggart (1921), 182
15 McTaggart (1921), 179
16 In my (1991)], I criticised McTaggart's argument, and tried to replace it with an argument for the weaker conclusion that the universe is a group of selves. But that weaker conclusion is not strong enough for my section 1.5 argument for the disseverality of selves.
17 Ignorance of the falsity of Colour Primitivism may be something that we prefer to knowledge of Ipseicism. Do we not love colour qualities and want them to be possessed by substances rather than dependent entities? The difficulty is that Colour Primitivism is consistent with the proposition that we do not know, of any substantial nonself, just what particular colour quality it has. Her eyes are blue and you admire them (they are a beautiful violet blue). And it is perhaps not easy to think that the blueness is just somehow in your experience as of her eyes, and hence not a property of her or of her eyes, but a property of you, her eyes being for all you know in reality greyish green. For more on what we want to be true about colours, see my (1986); (2001), ch. 5.

3 AT LEAST ONE TRANSCENDENT SELF

A transcendent self I defined as one that causes the existence of any non-abstract nonselves there may be which are not composed of selves, and causes the existence of all those selves which do not cause the existence of every other self.[1] In this chapter, I make an explanatory inference to the existence of at least one transcendent self. My inference relies on two principles. The first I call Exclusion. It says that for any non-empty class of entities, there is a causal explanation for the existence of all the members of that class if and only if their existence is caused by at least one non-member of that class. The second principle I call Evidential Sufficient Reason. It says that there is a causal explanation for p's truth if and only if there is no strong and undefeated evidence that there is no such explanation. Sections 3.1 and 3.2 are about why we should accept these two principles. They are put to work in sections 3.3 and 3.4. It emerges that they will not do the work required of them unless, as maintained in section 1.5, selves are disseveralities, which is to say unless each self has a constant quality which it does not share with any other substance.

3.1 Exclusion

Exclusion says that for any non-empty class of entities, there is a causal explanation for the existence of all the members of that class if and only if their existence is caused by at least one non-member of that class. By causing an entity to exist, I mean causing it to start existing if it has not always existed, and in any case causing it to continue to exist for as long as it does exist.

An explanation for the existence of all the members of the non-empty class of Fs is not quite the same as an explanation of why the class of Fs is non-empty, or of why there is at least one F, or of why there are any Fs at all. If the class of Fs has just two members, x and y, and if there is no explanation for the existence of x, then by explaining y's existence, we explain why the class of Fs is non-empty, and why there is at least one F, and why there are any Fs at all, but we do not explain the existence of all the members of

DOI: 10.4324/9781003274483-4

the class of Fs. To explain the existence of all the members of the class of F's is to leave the existence of none of its members unexplained. If a causal explanation for the existence of all the Fs requires there to be an entity which is not itself an F, so also does a causal explanation of why the class of Fs is non-empty, of why there is at least one F, and of why there are any F's at all. But I focus on the principle which I have called Exclusion because it is for the existence of at least one self an event in which causes the existence of *all* the substances of a certain class that I want to argue.

Why does a causal explanation for the existence of all the members of a class of entities require there to be an entity which is not itself a member of the class? Suppose that the class of F's has a finite number of members. If the whole membership of the class were caused by an F, then a member of the class would have to be caused by itself, which is absurd. What if there is an infinite number of F's, and each F belongs to an infinite series of F's, each member of which is caused to exist by an event belonging to its predecessor in the series? Should we not say, with Hume, that these particular causal explanations, none of which involves the existence of a non-F, add up to an explanation of the whole membership of the class of F's? Suppose that there is 'a chain ... or succession of objects, [and] each part is caused by that which preceded it, and causes that which succeeds it', and that it is claimed that the WHOLE still 'wants a cause'. According to Hume, 'the uniting of these parts into a whole, like the uniting of several distinct counties into one kingdom, or several distinct members into one body, is performed merely by an arbitrary act of mind, and has no influence on the nature of things. Did I show you the particular causes of each individual in a collection of twenty particles of matter, I should think it very unreasonable, should you afterwards ask me, what was the cause of the whole twenty. This is sufficiently explained in explaining the cause of the parts'.[2]

One might reply that there is no reason to suppose that the whole membership of the class of F's is just the product of an arbitrary act of mind. One might also reply that to suppose that each F is caused by another F is not to explain why there is a class of F's whose members are thus causally related rather than a class of entities of some other kind. A third answer has been supplied by Alexander Pruss.[3] Corresponding to the infinite series of F's, each caused to exist by its predecessor in the series, there would be an infinite series $p_1, p_2, \ldots$ of distinct propositions such that p_n is explained by p_{n+1}, and such that the conjunction of them all, $p_1 \& p_2 \& \ldots$, has thereby been explained. Let P indicate the conjunction of all these propositions. Let EVEN be the conjunction of the even numbered ones. Let ODD be the conjunction of the odd numbered ones. Every conjunct of EVEN then has an explanation in terms of ODD, since p_2 is explained by p_3, p_4 by p_5, and so on. So ODD has the resources for an explanation of EVEN, if we are dealing with a case in which the conjunction can be explained simply by giving explanations of the conjuncts. But by parallel reasoning, every conjunct of

ODD has an explanation in terms of EVEN, since p1 is explained by p2, p3 by p4, and so on. Thus we can explain EVEN in terms of ODD and ODD in terms of EVEN, which is absurd.

It does not of course follow from Exclusion that for any non-empty class of entities, there actually is a causal explanation for the existence of all the members of that class. Exclusion just says what else will be the case if there is indeed such an explanation. The principle is quite consistent with the existence of classes for whose whole membership there is no causal explanation. One such class is the class of all entities: a non-member of the class of entities is not an entity, and it is not consistent to suppose that a nonentity can be a cause. Given Exclusion, there is no explanation of why there is something rather than nothing. And if there are entities which are uncausable because they have neither a spatial nor a temporal location, or because they exist necessarily, then there is no causal explanation for all the members of a class to which such an entity belongs.

We may wonder what Exclusion implies about the causal relations between the members of classes whose whole membership is causally explained. Suppose that there is just one non-F, X, which causes the whole membership of the two-membered class of F's. Can it be true both that X causes the whole membership of the class of F's and that one of the F's causes the existence of the other? Indeed it can: Exclusion does not commit us to occasionalism. Let A and B be the two F's, and let eA be a change in A which is a sufficient cause of the event eB of B's coming into existence. Assume a regularity theory of causation, on which eA will be a sufficient cause of cause eB only if it is true that whenever there is an event like eA, it is followed by an event like eB, and certain other conditions are satisfied which do not postulate any primitively necessary connection between eA and eB. Now suppose that a change in X, eX, is also a sufficient cause of eB. To see that there is no inconsistency between 'eA is a sufficient cause of eB' and 'eX is a sufficient cause of eB', it is enough to recognize that there is no inconsistency between (i) 'Whenever there is an event like eA, it is followed by an event like eB' and (ii) 'Whenever there is an event like eX, it is followed by an event like eB'. Nor is there even an inconsistency between 'eA is a sufficient cause of eB' and 'eX is a necessary and sufficient cause of eB'. For 'Whenever there is an event like eA, there is a simultaneous event like eX' is consistent with 'When and only when there is an event like eX, there is an event like eB': it may be true that whenever there is an event like eA, there is a simultaneous event like eX. Nor will it follow that in this last case, eA causes eB indirectly, by way of causing eX. For there is a good argument for the principle that causes and effects cannot be simultaneous, and hence that eA does not cause eX at all. 'If simultaneous causation were possible – if A caused B simultaneously, and B caused C simultaneously – then, by Hume's principle [that "anything can produce anything"]...it would be logically possible that B could have had, instead of its normal effect, not-A. That logically impossible conjunction of causal sequences is, given Hume's principle, only rendered impossible if we suppose simultaneous causation itself to be impossible'.[4]

3.2 Evidential Sufficient Reason

The second explanatory principle which is needed in the argument for the existence of at least one transcendent self is Evidential Sufficient Reason (ESR). This says that for any true proposition p, there is a causal explanation for p's truth if and only if there is no strong and undefeated evidence that there is no such explanation.

ESR can be compared with a more familiar principle of sufficient reason which says that for any true proposition p, if 'there is a causal explanation for p's truth' is consistent, then there is a causal explanation for p's truth. This more familiar principle I will call SR. It may be that there are counterexamples to SR. If it is consistent to suppose that all human actions have an explanation, but there is strong and undefeated evidence that there are free human actions which have no explanation, then that tells against SR. But it does not tell against ESR.

If quantum mechanics tells us that some events, which it is consistent to suppose have explanations, in fact have no explanations then that tells against SR but not against ESR.

It is also true that if we combine SR with Exclusion, then absurdities follow, which do not afflict the combination of Exclusion with ESR. Exclusion says that for any non-empty class of entities, there is a causal explanation for the existence of all the members of that class if and only if their existence is caused by at least one non-member of that class. It is consistent to suppose that there is a causal explanation for the existence of all the non-unicorns. So by SR, there is such an explanation. But by Exclusion, there is a causal explanation for the existence of all the non-unicorns only if there is at least one unicorn. So, absurdly, there is at least one unicorn. But no such absurdity follows if we replace SR with ESR. If it is absurd to suppose that there are any unicorns, then that is strong and undefeated evidence that there are none. And ESR says that for any true proposition p, there is a causal explanation for p's truth only if there is no strong and undefeated evidence that there is no such explanation. So although it is consistent to say that there is a causal explanation for the existence of all the non-unicorns, and although by Exclusion such an explanation would have to postulate the existence of at least one unicorn, the combination of Exclusion with ESR does not commit us the acceptance of such an explanation.

It seems that sometimes when there is no strong and undefeated evidence that there is no causal explanation for the existence of all the entities of a certain class, the only available causal explanation postulates the existence of something unobservable. If ESR then requires us to believe in the existence of this unobservable something, then it is a principle which seems to collide with van Fraassen's constructive empiricism. Van Fraassen has suggested that if a scientific theory postulates unobservable entities, then we should accept it, if at all, not in the sense of believing that it is true, but only in the sense of believing that it is empirically adequate, where a theory is empirically adequate if and only if it tells the truth about what is observable. 'I hear scratching in the wall, the patter of little feet at midnight, my cheese disappears - and I infer that a mouse has come to live with me'. This pattern of inference need not lead us to belief in the existence of unobservable entities. Unlike sub-atomic particles, mice are observable.[5] Why should we thus restrict ourselves to the empirically adequate?

> If I believe the theory to be true and not just empirically adequate, my risk of being shown to be wrong is exactly the risk that the weaker entailed belief will conflict with actual experience. Meanwhile, by avowing the stronger belief, I place myself in the position of being able to answer more questions, of having a richer, fuller picture of the world, a wealth of opinion, so to say, that I can dole out to those who wonder. But since this extra opinion is not additionally vulnerable, the risk is - in human terms- illusory, and *therefore so is the wealth*. It is but empty strutting and posturing, this display of courage under fire and avowal of additional resources which cannot feel the pinch of misfortune. What can I do but express my disdain for this appearance of greater courage in embracing additional beliefs which will *ex hypothesi* never brave a more severe test?[6]

Mice are observable, but sub-atomic entities are not. But here there is a minefield. 'Externalists' suppose that I have mental contents entirely constituted by mind-independent entities. Is this true? Or is it rather that I infer from my experiences as of mind-independent entities that such entities exist? If the latter, I may also infer that there are mind-independent entities which closely resemble the contents of these experiences, such as mind-independent mice which closely resemble the contents of my experiences as of mice. But then why is that last inference more reliable than the inference from experience to the existence of the kind of entities that Van Fraassen counts as unobservable?

Why should we accept ESR? I offer two arguments for its truth, one simple, the other rather complex. The more complex argument begins with the assumption that ESR is true if the more general principle is true that for any true proposition p, there is an explanation for p's truth if and only if there is no strong and never to be defeated evidence that there is no such explanation. I then offer some support for this more general principle, which I call ESR*. Let Exp stand for 'there is an explanation for p's truth', and let Evp stand for 'there is strong and never to be defeated evidence for p'. Not Ev not-p will accordingly stand for 'there is no strong and never to be defeated evidence that p is false'. ESR* then says that for any true p, if not Ev not Exp, then Exp. Let H stand for the negation of ESR*, i.e., 'for some p, p & not Ev not-Exp, & not Exp'. And take, as a witnessing instance of H, H*:

'q & not Ev not Exq, & not Exq'. We now have the following argument for not H*, and hence for not H, and for ESR*.

(1) H*
(2) For all p, if p, then either not Ev not-Exp or Ev not-Exp
(3) Either not Ev not-ExH* or Ev not ExH* from (1) and (2)
(4) Ev not ExH*
(5) If H*, then Ev not ExH*
(6) Not H* from (1), (3), (4), (5)

Why (4)? If ExH*, then Ex(q & not Ev not-Exq, & not-Exq). Explanation is dissective: necessarily if there is an explanation for a conjunction, then there is an explanation for each of the conjuncts. So if ExH*, then (Exq and Ex not-Exq). But explanation is also factive: Exp entails p. So if ExH*, then (Exq and not-Exq). But not (Exq and not-Exq), and so not ExH*. But this reasoning provides strong and never to be defeated evidence for not ExH*, and so Ev not ExH*.

Why (5)? Suppose that H* and Ev not ExH*. If ExH*, then by the dissectiveness of explanation Exq & Ex not Ev not Exq, & Ex not Exq. So if Ev not ExH*, then either (i) Ev not-Exq, or (ii) Ev not Ex not Ev not Exq, or (iii) Ev not Ex not-Exq. If H*, then (i) is ruled out, because not Ev not Exq is an actual conjunct of H*. That leaves (ii) and (iii) to be ruled out. Suppose H* and (ii). Not Ev not Exq is an actual conjunct of H*, and if it is true, then it is unlikely to be the case that as (ii) says Ev not Ex not Ev not Exq. Finally, suppose that H* and (iii). According to (iii) Ev not Ex not Exq. But it is a conjunct of H* that not Exq. And it is implausible to say that if not Exq, then there is strong and undefeated evidence that there is no explanation for this explanatory absence. There is an explanation even for the absence of a causal explanation for the existence of beings, namely that by Exclusion there is a causal explanation for the existence of all the members of a class only if their existence is caused by at least one non-member of that class.

The simpler argument for ESR goes as follows. Define an alpha proposition as a true proposition such that there is no strong and undefeated evidence that there is no causal explanation for its truth. And let 'an alpha proposition p has an explanation' mean that there is a causal explanation for p's truth. We then have this.

(1) Many and varied alpha propositions are known to have causal explanations for their truth
(2) No alpha propositions are known not to have causal explanations for their truth

So probably

(3) All alpha propositions have causal explanations for their truth.

Plainly, (1) is true. (2) is true because if a proposition is an alpha proposition, then there is no strong and undefeated evidence that there is no causal explanation for its truth, from which it follows that it is not known that there is no causal explanation for its truth. And (3) is equivalent to ESR.

(1) and (2) yield probably (3) only if Induction is reliable, only if most of the time Induction yields true conclusions from true premises. And there are, of course, inductive sceptics, who deny that we can know that Induction is reliable. They will insist that there is no non-question-begging argument for the reliability of Induction, and that its reliability is not entailed by any true proposition of the form 'S is acquainted with x'. This strikes me as an unnecessary scruple. We do not need to *know* that Induction is reliable, any more than we need to know that there is a plurality of selves. For these are what we might call *consensual propositions*. A proposition is consensual if and only if (i) almost anyone who entertains it firmly believes it; (ii) almost anyone who entertains (i) firmly believes (i); (iii) almost anyone who entertains (ii) firmly believes (ii); and so on, ad infinitum. I think that if a proposition is thus consensual, and one believes it, then reflection will destroy any desire one may have to know that it is true. Why so? The answer can be found in Excursus B.

3.3 An Explanatory Inference

From the existence of non-abstract entities which are not transcendent selves, we can infer with the help of our two explanatory principles that there is at least one transcendent self. Non-abstract entities which are not transcendent selves are either nonselves, or selves which are not transcendent. But a group of selves is a nonself. So therefore is a group of selves which includes at least one transcendent self, and we cannot expect the postulation of at least one transcendent self to explain why there is a group of selves of which a transcendent self is a member. Let me say then that the entities from whose existence we can infer that there is at least one transcendent self are beta entities, where a beta entity is a non-abstract entity which is either a non-transcendent self or a nonself of which no component is a transcendent self. With E standing for Exclusion, and ESR standing for Evidential Sufficient Reason, we now have this argument:

(1) There are beta-entities
(2) E
(3) ESR
(4) If there are beta-entities, then there is no strong and undefeated evidence that there is no causal explanation for the existence of them all
(5) There is a causal explanation for the existence of all the beta-entities [from (1), (4) and ESR]
(6) There is at least one non-member of the class of beta-entities which causes all the beta-entities to exist [from (5) and E]
(7) There is at least one transcendent self [from (6)].

The conclusion of this argument follows from its premises. (7) follows from (6) because a non-member of the class of beta entities is either (i) a self or (ii) a nonself. If (i) it is a transcendent self, and if (ii), then either (a) it has at least one transcendent self as a component, which makes (7) true, or (b) it is an abstract entity, which is excluded because only a non-abstract entity can cause anything to exist. Is the argument (1) – (7) sound as well as valid? (1) is true if only because non-transcendent selves exist. (2) and (3) were justified in sections 3.1 and 3.2. What of premise (4)?

To (4) someone may object that it must be false if (1), (2) and (3) are true. For (6) follows from (1) – (4), and (6) is false. A transcendent self is a self which causes the existence of all the beta-entities. But how can a self cause anything except through the mediacy of its already existing body? And if a body is a nonself of which no component is a transcendent self, then a body is a beta entity, and however many beta-entities there are which a self causes to exist, there is one which, since its existence is already required for there to be such causation, cannot be caused to exist by that self. Another difficulty is that it is by no means clear that a bodiless transcendent self cannot cause the existence of the beta entities just by fiat. Wittgenstein wrote that 'only of a human being and what resembles (behaves like) a living human being can one say: it has sensations; it sees; is blind; is deaf; *is conscious or unconscious*'.[7] His followers have taken this to imply that psychological predicates cannot be meaningfully ascribed to a bodiless entity.[8] In that case, a bodiless entity cannot issue a fiat. I shall assume, however, this doctrine about psychological predicates is mistaken.

(1) – (7) is an argument for the existence of at least one transcendent self. It tells us nothing about just how many such selves there are. Could it be that the only transcendent self is the one God of Judaism or Islam? Or that the only transcendent selves are the three Persons of the Christian Trinity? Reasoning might be attempted from which the answers to these questions would fall out. But as I said in the Introduction, I do not attempt it here.

It could seem that just by accepting the principle of ESR, I am committed to a richer conclusion about the number of the transcendent selves than there is at least one. I am committed to the conclusion that they are infinite in number. One may at this point seem to hear the voice of Schopenhauer. To say that every event has a cause, and yet insist on the existence of an uncaused cause, is, he thought, to treat the causal principle as a hired cab to be dismissed once one has reached one's destination. Is this not how I am treating ESR? Suppose there is just one transcendent self x. ESR says that for any true proposition p, there is an explanation for p's truth if and only if there is no strong and undefeated evidence that there is no such explanation. But surely there is no strong and undefeated evidence that there is no causal explanation for the existence of this transcendent self x. And so by ESR, there is such an explanation. The existence of a transcendent self can hardly be explained by the fiat of a non-transcendent self, and a transcendent self cannot be caused to exist by a non-abstract nonself. So the existence of the transcendent self x is caused by a further transcendent self. And now the reasoning can be repeated. Surely there is no strong and undefeated evidence that there is no causal explanation for the existence of whatever further transcendent self explains the existence of x. There is, then, at least one further transcendent self which explains the existence of whatever transcendent self explains the existence of x. And then again there is surely no strong and undefeated evidence that there is no causal explanation for the existence of whatever transcendent self explains the existence of whatever transcendent self explains the existence of whatever transcendent self explains the existence of x, and so there is at least one further transcendent self which...and so on, ad infinitum. It may seem then that we are committed to the existence of an infinite number of transcendent selves, each of which is caused to exist by at least one other transcendent self.

Consider, however, the assumptions here being made about the absence of strong and undefeated evidence. Suppose a sound argument exists for the truth of an ostensibly revealed religion whose doctrines imply that just one transcendent self exists. Then x will be this one transcendent self, and there will after all be strong and undefeated evidence that there is no further transcendent self x1 which explains why x exists. The strong and undefeated evidence that there is no further transcendent self x1 which explains why x exists will be provided by the argument for the truth of the ostensibly revealed religion. I do not try to show, of any ostensibly revealed religion, that there really is a strong argument for its truth. The point is only that until we know that there is no strong argument for the truth of any ostensibly revealed religion which teaches what implies that there is only a finite number of transcendent selves, we cannot claim that ESR commits us to the doctrine that they are infinite in number.

3.4 The Causation of Disseveralities

Suppose that, in the argument (1) – (7), (4) is true, and that the argument is sound. What, in that case, prevents us from arguing as follows?

(8) There are selves
(9) Exclusion (E)
(10) Evidential Sufficient Reason (ESR)
(11) If there are selves, then there is no strong and undefeated evidence that there is no causal explanation for the existence of them all
(12) There is a causal explanation for the existence of all the selves [from (8), (11) and ESR]
(13) There is at least one non-member of the class of selves which causes the existence of all the selves [from E and (12)]
(14) There is at least one non-abstract nonself which causes all the selves to exist [from (13)]

(8) – (14) is as valid as (1) – (7). (8) is as incontestable as (1). (9) and (10) are the same as (2) and (3). (11), it may seem, is no less true than (4). (1), (2), (3) and (4) together entail (6). And (8), (9), (10) and (11) together entail (13). But (6) is incompatible with (13), and so the two arguments (1) – (7) and (8) – (14) cannot both be sound. There is, it seems, no reason to believe that there is at least one transcendent self unless (1) – (7) is sound and (8) – (14) is unsound. But it may also seem that there is no more reason to believe that (1) – (7) is sound and (8) – (14) unsound than there is to believe that (8) – (14) is sound and (1) – (7) unsound.

Is (6) really incompatible with (13)? It is. From (6) it follows that there is at least one transcendent self which explains the existence of all the beta-entities. A beta-entity is a non-abstract entity which is either a transcendent self or a nonself of which no component is a transcendent self. So from (6) it follows that there is at least one transcendent self which explains the existence of all non-abstract nonselves of which no transcendent self is a component. Now from (13) it follows that the existence of all the selves is explained by at least one non-abstract nonself. But we cannot expect a nonself to explain the existence of all the selves if this nonself has either a transcendent or a nontranscendent self as one of its own components. And it cannot be the case that, as (6) says, the existence of the non-abstract nonselves of which no transcendent self is a component is explained by a transcendent self if, as (13) implies, the existence of this transcendent self is itself explained by a nonself of which no transcendent self is a component.

The best way out, I think, is to reject (11). Contrary to (11), there *is* strong and undefeated evidence that there is no causal explanation for the existence of all the selves. Given Exclusion, there would be a causal explanation for the existence of all the selves only if they were caused to exist by a nonself which was not composed of selves. But I think it can be shown that even if there are indeed non-abstract nonselves which are not composed of selves, still no such entity can cause the existence of a disseverality. If that is right, then, given Exclusion, (11) falls, and with it the argument (8) – (14). For selves are disseveralities, in the sense that no self shares its ipseical quality with any other substance. And I think it can be shown that no disseverality can be caused to exist by a non-abstract nonself not composed of selves.

To give a causal explanation for the existence of a substance, it is necessary to deduce that it exists, or that it is highly probable that it exists, from a true conjunction such that (i) one conjunct is a generalisation, (ii) the other conjunct is a singular proposition asserting the occurrence of a particular event, of a type referred to by the generalisation, and (iii) neither of these conjuncts by itself entails that the explanandum exists or that it is highly probable that it exists. For the explanation to be causal, the conjunction must doubtless satisfy further conditions, among them perhaps that the generalisation should be in some way law-like. But for present purposes, I need not specify any condition on the conjunction other than the tripartite condition just mentioned. I suggest that if a substance is a disseverality, then the only conjunction which meets this tripartite condition, and from which we can deduce the existence of that substance, is one in which the generalisation is about mental events, and in which the singular proposition asserts the occurrence of a mental event. If this is right, then since selves are disseveralities, we can move quite easily to the further conclusion that the existence of a self cannot be causally explained by a non-abstract nonself not composed of selves, and hence to the rejection of (11).

Let x be a substance which is not a disseverality and which has a property G. If you like, x is a substance of which a G-trope is a constituent. In our efforts to give a causal explanation of why this G-type substance x exists, we may appeal *inter alia* to a generalisation about the conditions under which *any* G-type substance exists. We may appeal, for example, to the generalisation that a G-type substance will exist at some time if 10 seconds earlier there was an F-type event, or to the generalisation that a G-type substance will exist at some spatio-temporal position if there is an F-type event whose spatio-temporal position bears relation R to the spatio-temporal position of that G-type substance. But now suppose that x is a disseverality with the disseveral property G*. Then there is no other substance with the property G*: x is the *only* G*-type substance. And so we cannot give a causal explanation of why this solitary G*-type substance exists by appealing *inter alia* to a generalisation about the conditions under which *any* G*-type substance exists. Since there is just one G*-type substance, no such generalisation will be true.

How then can we give a causal explanation for the existence of this solitary G*-type substance? To what generalisation can we appeal? The generalisation must, I think, be one which links mental events to the actualisation of their intentional contents. Suppose that there is a self S such that whenever S wills that something is so, then that something is so. Conjoin this generalisation about the efficacy of S's volitions with the singular proposition that S wills that the disseveral substance x exists, and you have a conjunction which entails that x exists. And since neither of the conjuncts by itself entails that x exists, you have here a causal explanation of x's existence, or at any rate a conjunction which satisfies the above-mentioned tripartite condition for a causal explanation. The explanatory generalisation is not about all the particulars which are qualitatively identical to the explanandum. Rather, the explanatory generalisation is about all the events which are similar to the cause, namely all those volitions of S whose intentional content is that something is so. It is not necessary to suppose that, as in this example, the explanatory generalisation is about volitions, and that the singular proposition refers to a volition. It would do just as well if the generalisation were about what is so when S wants something to be so, and the singular proposition were that S wants x to exist. Equally, the generalisation may be probabilistic, and the explanandum may be only that there is a high probability that x exists. The essential thing is that the explanation is one in which the generalisation links mental entities to the actualisation of their intentional contents, and that the singular proposition is that there is a mental event either with the intentional content that the explanandum exists or with the intentional content that there is a high probability that it exists. If x is a self and so a disseverality, then if its existence has a causal explanation, this can only be a mental explanation of the kind just described. And from this it will follow that the existence of a particular self cannot be causally explained by a non-abstract nonself not composed of selves. The existence of a self could be causally explained by a non-abstract nonself not composed of selves only if the mental entity which explained it were dependent on a substantial nonself not composed of selves. But mental entities depend on selves, not on nonselves not composed of selves. So if we assume Exclusion, and grant that we are selves, then, contrary to premise (11) of the argument (8) – (14), there is strong and undefeated evidence that there is no causal explanation for the existence of all the selves. (8) – (14) therefore falls, and fails to threaten the argument (1) – (7) for the existence of at least one transcendent self.

Someone may now suggest that no substance shares its properties with any other substance, so that if my reasoning is correct we have to embrace the absurd conclusion that the existence even of a substantial nonself not composed of selves is causally inexplicable by a non-abstract nonself. I reply that there is no reason to suppose no substance shares its properties with any other substance. Selves are disseveralities because they are many, and the best way to distinguish them from each other is to postulate differences between their ipseical qualities. But if there are substantial nonselves which are not composed of selves, then they may be spatial, and since no two particulars can occupy the same spatio-temporal position, there may perfectly well be a plurality of qualitatively indistinguishable substantial nonselves, none composed of selves and each individuated by its spatio-temporal position. We could give a causal explanation of why a particular G-type substantial nonself exists at spatio-temporal position sty by deducing the explanandum from a generalisation about all G-type particulars together with a singular proposition. The generalisation might be that if an F-type event occurs, then just one G-type particular exists at a spatio-temporal position to which the spatio-temporal position of the F-type event bears relation R. And the singular proposition might be that an F-type event occurred at a spatio-temporal position which bears R to sty. Needless to say, the mentalist kind of causal explanation, which is the only kind of causal explanation available for the existence of a particular self, may also be available for the existence of a particular substantial nonself not composed of selves, if there is such an entity.

It is one thing to explain why a particular self exists when it does, another to explain why, at some particular time, some self or other exists. I do not deny that to explain why some self or other exists at a particular time, we can perfectly well appeal to a generalisation of the form 'if an F-type event occurs at t, then 10 seconds later some self or other will exist', where an F-type event may be a non-mental event. But in the argument (1) – (7), premise (4) is about the explanation of the existence of each one of the beta-entities, and hence about the explanation of the existence of each particular non-transcendent self.

According to the principle of the Dissimilarity of the Diverse, different particulars have different properties. In section 1.5, I defended this principle against Richard Swinburne's contention that particulars may differ not in their properties but just in their thisness. For Swinburne souls, and hence persons have thisness, 'that is, for any person having any particular conjunction of intrinsic and relational properties, there could-it is logically possible – exist instead of that person any one of innumerable different persons with exactly the same (intrinsic and relational) properties'. Now 'laws of nature do not concern individual things as such; they concern individual things only insofar as they have certain properties'.[9] Laws of nature are principles which determine relations between substances which depend on their properties; 'they determine that all events consisting of a substance having a certain conjunction of properties cause an event of that substance or a substance related to it in certain ways to have certain properties, or cause the existence of a substance with certain properties, or cause a substance with certain properties to cease to exist'.[10] It follows that there cannot be a full scientific explanation of the existence of any particular soul. From the doctrine that souls have thisness, Swinburne derives a negative conclusion which would be as serviceable in defence of my argument (1) – (7) for the existence of at least one transcendent self as the negative conclusion which I derived from the doctrine that selves are disseveralities, my conclusion, namely, that no non-abstract nonself not composed of selves can cause the existence of a disseverality. To explain the existence of a particular self, one must, so I argued, appeal to a generalisation which links mental events to the actualisation of their intentional contents, and so accept the existence of the further self or selves on which these mental events depend. How does Swinburne think that we can explain the existence of particular souls? We are to postulate the action of an omnipotent God. 'Knowing the essence of each of us' God 'will know the difference between creating me and creating someone else. Souls do not differ from each other by virtue of having different necessary properties, and since before they are created they cannot have any contingent properties "hard" properties, that is, properties which belong to them by virtue of how things are with them at that time), there will be no property of either of us which could provide God with a reason for creating me rather than someone else...; and God is not subject to non-rational desires in favour of one choice rather than another. But this is a familiar situation for all rational beings, when faced with equally good incompatible alternatives, and subject to no non-rational desires'.[11] A choice between different disseveralities would on the other hand be a choice between different qualities, based on reasons hidden from us.

3.5 Essence and Existence

A further difficulty must be confronted before we can affirm on the basis of (1) – (7) that at least one transcendent self exists. Scholastic philosophers have argued that there exists at least one non-abstract entity whose essence is its existence and which causes the existence of all those entities whose essence is distinct from their existence. They have argued, as we can say, for the existence of at least one E=E entity which causes the existence of all E+E entities. (1) – (7) seems to show that there is at least one transcendent self which causes all the beta entities to exist, where a beta entity is defined as a non-abstract entity which is either a non-transcendent self or a nonself of which no component is a transcendent self. Is an E=E entity a beta entity? Surely not: an entity whose essence is its existence can hardly be caused to exist by something else. Is an E=E entity a transcendent self? How can it be, if the essence of an E=E entity is its existence, and the essence of a self is a disseveral quality? It seems, then, that either there is fatal flaw in the argument (1) – (7) or, *pace* the scholastic philosophers, there is no such thing as an E=E entity. I will not try to escape from this dilemma by maintaining that E=E entities are, after all, somehow transcendent selves. Nor will I abandon the argument (1) – (7). Instead, I will try to fault what seem to be the most plausible arguments for the existence of at least one E=E entity. Two arguments suggest themselves, one from causation, the other from existence. I will look at them in the remaining two sections of the present chapter.

3.6 An Argument from Causation

The first argument that I want to consider for the existence of an E=E entity is from causation. It starts like this.

(1) Every E+E entity is caused to exist by some other entity
(2) There cannot be an infinite series of E+E entities each of which is caused to exist by the next member of the series
(3) Every E+E entity is caused to exist by at least one E=E entity.

More would of course be needed to show that every E+E entity is caused to exist by the same E=E entity or entities.

Consider to begin with the principle:

(P1) One entity causes another to exist only if it does not share the responsibility for doing that with any other entity.

Given (P1), (2) is true: there cannot be an infinite series of E+E entities each of which is caused to exist by the next member of the series. There cannot even be a series of three E+E entities in which the second causes the existence of the first and the third the existence of the second. (1) says that every E+E entity is caused to exist by another entity. If y is an entity which causes the existence of an E+E entity x, then by (1) and (P1), y cannot be an E+E entity. If every E+E entity is caused to exist by another entity, and y is an E+E entity, then y is caused to exist by another entity, and in this case, contrary to P1, y's responsibility for causing the existence of x is shared with that other entity. So if every E+E entity is caused to exist by another entity, and an E+E entity x is caused to exist by y, then y can only be an E=E entity. The difficulty, of course, is that if you do insist on (P1), insist that one entity causes the existence of another only if it does not share the responsibility for doing that with any other entity, then you will be at a loss to say why we should accept that, as (1) says, every E+E entity is caused to exist by some other entity.

Abandoning (P1), you might suggest instead that

(P2) one entity causes the existence of another only if it is true that only given the existence of the former entity *can* the latter entity exist.

It may seem that if (P2) is true, then that is enough to make it true that

(2) There cannot be an infinite series of E+E entities each of which is caused to exist by the next member of the series.

It may seem that, given (P2), it would be incoherent to suppose that there is infinite series of entities each of which after the first causes the existence of its predecessor. Given (P2), there would be no end to the series of necessary conditions which would have to be satisfied in order for it to be even possible for the first member of the series to exist. And if it could never be unconditionally true that the first member *can* exist, then it can never be unconditionally true that the first member *does* exist. But if you insist on (P2), with its stringent *can*, then, as before, you will be at a loss to say why we should accept, with (1), that every E+E entity is caused to exist by another entity. And (P2) will in any case be difficult to insist on if, as the discussion in Excursus A may incline you to suppose, the only intelligible primitive modal terms are those used to describe our experiences of a two-way ability to decide. For how, in that case, can a meaning be found for the *can* in (P2)?

Abandoning (P2), you might invoke the notion of an *instrument*. Consider an infinite series of E+E entities, A1, A2, A3,..., in which each member is caused to exist by the next member of the series: A1 is caused to exist by A2, A2 is caused to exist by A3, and so on. You may think that (i) it is natural to regard each member of the series after A1 as the instrument of the member which succeeds it: A2 is used by A3 as an instrument to cause the existence of A1, A3 is used by A4 as an instrument to cause the existence of A2, and so on. But then you may think that (ii) there cannot be an *infinite* series in which each member after the first is used by the

At Least One Transcendent Self

next member as an instrument to cause the existence of its predecessor. For there cannot be an end or goal and an infinite series of instruments in which each member after the first is used as an instrument by the previous member to achieve that goal. A series in which members after the first are used as instruments on their predecessors must come to an end, and its last member must be succeeded by an agent who is not used as an instrument to achieve that goal. And so you may conclude that there cannot be an infinite series of E+E entities in which each member is caused to exist by another member: a series of E+E entities each of which is caused to exist by something else must have a last member which is caused to exist by something which is not an E+E entity caused to exist by another E+E entity, but rather an agent which is either (a) not caused to exist by any other entity or (b) an E=E entity. Since (a) is excluded by (1), the first premise of (1) – (3), we are left with (b), and hence with (3). A homely illustration of the principle (ii) is provided by Thomas Crean, in the course of a defence of Aquinas's First Way. 'Consider someone who is peeling potatoes. It's not self-contradictory to suppose that he has been peeling potatoes forever, and has by now amassed an infinitely large heap of them. From time to time, his potato peeler becomes rusty, and so he throws it aside and takes up a new one. It's not self-contradictory to suppose that he has by now amassed an infinitely large pile of rusty potato peelers. What would be impossible is that, to peel any given potato, an infinite multitude of implements should have to be used together, each one acting on the next. If, in order to peel any given potato, the potato peeler in contact with it had to be turned by another peeler, and this other by a third and so on without end, then one would never reach the man himself. If each instrument had to be put in action by another instrument, one would never reach the principal cause. But in that case, the potato would never be peeled'.[12]

I do not think that this reasoning works. '(i) it is natural to regard each member of the series after A1 as the instrument of the member which succeeds it' needs to be replaced by '(i)* each member of the series after A1 *is* the instrument of the member which succeeds it'. And then we must ask, Why suppose that (i)*? An instrument requires a conscious agent, like the man who peels the potatoes. But that one E+E entity causes the existence of another does not, by itself, imply that there is any such thing as a conscious agent.

Leaving aside the notion of an instrument, you might now invoke the notion of a *power*. You might claim that in an infinite series of E+E entities A1, A2, A3..., in which each member is caused to exist by the next member, each member of the series after A1 would have a power, derived from its successor, to cause the existence of its predecessor. A2 would have a power derived from A3 to cause the existence of A1, A3 would have a power derived from A4 to cause the existence of A2, and so on, ad infinitum. But this, you might then claim, is not possible. Why, though, should we suppose it to be impossible? Just why must a series of entities each of which derives its power from another entity come to an end and be succeeded by an entity whose power is underived and from whose power the other entities in the series derive their powers? However exactly this question is answered, the answer will not stand up unless 'power' in 'x has the power to cause —' has an actual meaning. And if 'power', here, does have a meaning, then either it is a primitive and unanalysable modal term or its meaning can be captured in non-modal terms. I do not know of any non-modal analysis of 'power' in 'x has the power to cause —', which will make it plain that the infinite regress is impossible. And I doubt whether 'power', here, is a primitive but meaningful modal term. Sometimes I have an experience of having a two-way ability or power to decide. Though unanalysable, 'power', here, is, thanks to the experience, meaningful. But my power to decide is a human power, and there seems not to be any experience on the basis of which one could attribute an unanalysable power to a non-human E+E entity. This brings us back to the restrictive doctrine about the meaningfulness of primitive modal terms which I affirmed in section 1.6. As promised in that section, there will be some more about the restriction in Excursus A.

The argument (1) – (3) has affinities both with the one that Aquinas offers for *esse tantum* in chapter 4 of his *De Ente et Essentia* and with the Second Way of the *Summa Theologiae*. So one may wonder if it can be made to work with the help of the scholastic distinction, made use of by Aquinas, between an essentially or per se ordered causal series and a causal series ordered accidentally or per accidens. Is it the case that, unlike an accidentally ordered causal series, an essentially ordered causal series has to terminate? And is it the case that each E+E entity is caused to exist by another entity in a sense which makes it a member of an essentially ordered causal series?

Scotus gives this explanation of the difference between the two kinds of series. 'In essentially ordered causes, the second depends upon the first precisely in its act of causation. In accidentally ordered causes this is not the case, although the second may depend upon the first for its existence or in some other way. Thus a son depends on his father for his existence but is not dependent on him in exercising his own causality, since he can act just as well whether his father be living or dead'.[13] What is the meaning of 'In essentially ordered causes, the second depends on the first precisely in its act of causation.'?

Edward Feser invites us to consider 'the stock example of a hand which moves a stick which in turn moves a stone. The stick causes the stone to move, but not under its own power. It moves the stone only insofar as it is being used by the hand to move it. The hand (or, more properly, the person whose hand it is) is what Scholastics would call the *principal* cause of the stone's motion, with the stick being the *instrumental* cause. The stick has the power to move the stone only in a derivative or "secondary" way, and in that sense "depends on the first [i.e. the hand] precisely in its act of causation". That sort of dependence is the defining feature of an essentially ordered series of causes. There is an essential connection between the members of the series qua members insofar as the members lower down in the series have their causal power for as long as the series exists, only in so far as they derive it from a member higher up'.[14] Feser supposes that an essentially ordered causal series of E+E entities has to terminate. If that is right, and if every E+E entity is in the appropriate sense caused to exist by some other entity, then an essentially ordered causal series of E+E entities would have to be followed by an E = E entity. But an essentially ordered causal series of E+E entities does not have to terminate unless, contrary to what I suggested in the last paragraph but one, there cannot be an infinite series of E+E entities in which each member after the first is caused to exist by the next member, and each member after the first derives from its successor its power to cause the existence of its predecessor.

3.7 An Argument from Existence

The other argument that I want to consider for the existence of an E=E entity comes from the heroic and ingenious Australian philosopher Barry Miller. Defining a concrete entity as one which can either effect a real change or undergo a real change or both, and a concrete individual as one for which there is a distinction between it and its existence, Miller upholds an analysis of existence which entails that it is impossible for a concrete individual to exist without being caused, and caused, at least ultimately, by an E=E entity.[15]

Let 'Fido' be the name of a concrete individual. Many people would say that the truth of 'Fido exists' commits us by itself to the existence of no entity other than Fido. Miller disagrees. He thinks that 'Fido exists' is an atomic proposition, a proposition composed merely of a singular term and a simple predicate, and that its truth commits us to the existence of Subsistent Existence. He thinks that the ontological categories exemplified in Fido's existing are to be assigned in accordance with the linguistic categories of the expressions in the proposition made true by it, namely 'Fido exists'. On this view, Fido is an individual because he has a name, and existence is a property because a predicate stands for it, and Fido's existence is a property instance individuated by Fido. Fido and his instance of existence are then constituents of Fido's existing, i.e., it is from them that Fido's existing is conceptually constructible. But according to Miller, we now have a dilemma. There seems to be no starting point for such a construction. Fido's existence is disqualified because it is individuated by Fido. But Fido is disqualified because in respect of actuality, he is logically posterior to his instance of existence. Miller thinks that to resolve the dilemma, we must suppose that Fido has the capacity to individuate his existence by virtue of something, *a*, other than his existing. This means that 'Fido exists' is elliptical. And if by a cause we mean a necessary condition, then an acceptable expansion of the ellipsis is 'Fido exists inasmuch as Fido is caused to do so

74 At Least One Transcendent Self

by something external to him'. Do we now have an infinite causal series, in which Fido is caused to exist by an entity *a* external to him, and *a* is caused to exist by a third entity external to both Fido and *a*, and this third entity is caused to exist by a fourth entity external to Fido, *a* and the third entity, and so on ad infinitum? Or is it rather that either *a*, or the third entity if there is one, or the fourth entity if there is one, or ..., must be a concrete entity which is not an individual, i.e., is an entity which is not distinct from its existence? It is for the second alternative that Miller argues. Here is an outline of his argument.

(a) Every causal series has a linguistic expression which is causally explanatory
(b) The linguistic expression of a causal series is causally explanatory if it is closed and categorical
(c) The linguistic expression of a series of causes of F's existing requires the use of reduplicative expressions
(d) The linguistic expression of a series of causes of F's existing will not be closed and categorical unless it terminates [from (c)]
(e) The linguistic expression of a series of causes of F's existing terminates [from (b) and (d)]
(f) F's existing has an uncaused cause [from (e)]
(g) An uncaused cause is not distinct from its existence

Why (a)? Because it is part of the concept of a causal series that there is an account of the series which shows how it explains the effect with which the series begins.

Why (b)? 'An expression is closed and categorical' means that either it as a whole or some part of it is a closed and categorical sentence. A sentence is closed if it contains no unquantified variables. Thus 'the truck is moved by –' is an open sentence, and 'there is an x such that the truck is moved by x' is a closed sentence. 'Among closed sentences, only categorical ones (as opposed, e.g., to commands, questions and hypotheticals) are explanatory'.[16]

Why (c)? A reduplicative expression is one in which 'one of the terms is qualified in such a way as to express a necessary condition of the truth of the proposition expressed by it'.[17] 'F exists' is an elliptical expression whose expansion is the reduplicative 'F exists inasmuch as it is caused to do so by something *a* external to it', or 'F exists *qua* conditional on *a*'.

Why (d)? If F exists inasmuch as it is caused to do so by something *a* external to F, then it is also true that *a* exists inasmuch as it is caused to do so by something *b* external to *a*, and so on. And so, if F exists, then F is (inasmuch as *a* is ...) caused to exist by *a*. But 'F is (inasmuch as *a* is ...) caused to exist by *a*' is not a closed categorical expression. Nor is 'F is [inasmuch as *a* is (inasmuch as *b* is ...) caused to exist by *b*] caused to exist by *a*'. So if the linguistic expression of the series is causally explanatory, it cannot be expanded in this way forever, but must sooner or later terminate in a closed expression, such as 'F is (inasmuch as a is caused to exist by m) caused to exist by a'. m will then have to be a cause which does not exist only inasmuch as it is caused by something external to it.

Why (g)? Since m is uncaused, and since every entity which is distinct from its existence exists only inasmuch as it is caused to exist by something external to it, m must be an entity which is not distinct from its existence.

Miller has a further argument for the conclusion that there is just one such entity. Assume that in addition to m there is another uncaused cause n. 'Then since an uncaused cause is subsistent existence, m and n would be two instances of subsistent existence. But to say that they are two is to say that they are individuated, each being an individual instance of subsistent existence. But, if they are individuated, then m and n must each be distinct from its existence. But to say that would be to embrace a contradiction; for it would be saying that something which *cannot* be distinct from its existence (because uncaused) *is* distinct from its existence (because an individual). It is impossible therefore that there can be more than one uncaused cause. Cause m is not merely *an* uncaused cause, it is *the* uncaused cause – the ultimate cause not only of Fido's existing but of that of every other individual as well'.[18]

Suppose that there is no incoherence in the notion of an E=E entity. Would Miller's argument then be sound? Existence, for Miller, is a real property of individuals. So, 'in an existing Socrates, there are two distinct but inseparable elements, one being the Socrates element and the other the existential element - the instance of existence - without which Socrates would of course be quite bereft of actuality. The upshot is that the Socrates element has emerged as having no actuality whatsoever in its own right.... [But] surely there can be no instance of a property without there being something for it to be a property of'. Surely the individual is prior to its property instance not just with respect to individuation but with respect to actuality. According to Miller, this is 'by far and away the most powerful objection to existence being a real property'.[19] His reply is to insist that although Socrates is indeed logically posterior to his instance of existence, this is perfectly compatible with his being logically prior to his instance of existence in respect of individuation. This we are to see with the help of an analogy. A block of butter has been cut into a number of parts. Each piece of butter has a different surface or bound. Despite their ontological poverty, these bounds serve to individuate the pieces they bound. Socrates as it were bounds his instance of existence.[20] Nor is it true that the existence of Socrates, like the wisdom of Socrates, inheres in Socrates. Unlike his wisdom, his existence does not inhere in him, but is bounded by him.

There are of course other objections to Miller's doctrine of existence as a real property. One is that it collides with an ontology of pure particularism, for which, as I suggested in section 1.6, there is much to be said. For Miller, Fido's existence is a property instance individuated by Fido. But for the pure particularist, properties are universals, and universals are reducible to sets or sums of exactly resembling tropes. An instance of a property P is either one of the tropes to which that property is reducible or a compound substance whose diverse and compresent components include such a trope. I do not see how a property of existence can be reduced to a set or sum of exactly resembling existences or existence tropes, or how Fido, a compound substance, can have an existence trope as one of his components.

There are objections, of course, to pure particularism. But let me question what seem to be the two leading objections to that doctrine.

(i) Suppose that there are three particular rednesses, F, G, and H, which exactly resemble each other. It is alleged that to explain these resemblances, one must postulate three further particular relations, R1, R2 and R3, respectively holding between the pairs F and G, G and H, and F and H. But R1, R2, and R3 will also exactly resemble each other, and so one must postulate yet further particular and exactly resembling relations R4, R5 and R6, respectively holding between the pairs R1 and R2, R2 and R3, and R1 and R3 and so on ad infinitum. The regress seems vicious, either because it requires there to be an actual infinity of particular relations, or because we are at no stage any further towards an explanation of what it is for there to be an exact resemblance between particulars.

It may be replied that resemblance is not an entity over and above the entities that it is supposed to relate. Ontologically, it is, as Maurin puts it, a mere 'pseudo-addition'. If F, G, and H do indeed exactly resemble each other, no further particulars R1, R2 and R3 need to be postulated. Alternatively, exact resemblance is a mere internal relation, and the truth-makers for an internal relation are nothing more than the terms of the relation.

(ii) The second objection to pure particularism is inspired by Bradley. Suppose that the tropes X and Y are compresent constituents of a single object. Compresence seems not to be a mere pseudo-addition. It seems in fact to be an external relation. But if compresence is an external relation, then the tropist will have to say that the relation of compresence between X and Y is itself a trope. Call that trope C. Is C compresent with both X and Y? If not, then it cannot unify X and Y. But if so, then there are further relations of compresence, in which C is a term, and so yet further tropes. And so on ad infinitum. The regress is vicious, either because it requires there to be an actual infinity of tropes, or because at no stage are we any further towards an explanation of what it is for tropes to be unified in the objects that they compose. It may be replied, with Maurin,[21] that if compresence is an external relation, and C is a trope which unifies X and Y, then it can unify X and Y without itself being compresent with them. If compresence is an external relation, then it is not a mere pseudo-addition to the particulars which it unifies. But if a compresence trope does exist, then it is ontologically dependent on the particulars which it unifies. So if in an effort to explain the unification of the 'ordinary' tropes X and Y we postulate a compresence trope C, we are not postulating an entity whose existence gives rise to exactly the same kind of question about unification. Even if there are actual infinities, the postulation of an infinity of unified 'ordinary' tropes cannot explain the unification of the 'ordinary' tropes X and Y. But if actual infinities are not ruled out, then because compresence tropes are not 'ordinary' tropes, the postulation of an infinite number of compresence basic particulars can explain the unification of two ordinary basic particulars.

On the assumption that there is no incoherence in the notion of an E=E entity, Miller's argument for the existence of such an entity is hard to fault. I do not think that there is a conclusive objection to his doctrine that Fido's existence is a property instance individuated by Fido. The most plausible attempt to vindicate the coherence of the notion of an E=E entity is it seems Miller's own. I do not think it works.

According to Miller, there is 'no problem in maintaining that Subsistent Existence is an entity in which its quiddity = its existence, or an entity in which what exists = its existence. The reason is simply that the left-hand side of these claims is to be understood as "the limit case bound of existence" and the right-hand side by "the limit case instance of existence". Hence, the claims translate into the following:

The *limit case* bound of existence = the *limit case* instance of existence

This would be self-contradictory only if it implied:

Some bound of existence = the instance of existence which it bounds'

Now we need the notion of an alienans adjective. In 'rocking horse', 'rocking' is an alienans adjective: a rocking horse is not a horse at all. "Limit case" is also an alienans adjective: a limit case bound is not a bound at all, nor is a limit case instance of existence an instance of existence. 'Consequently, there is no difficulty in maintaining that the very same entity is both the limit case bound of existence and the limit case instance of existence'.[22]

A limit case is to be distinguished from a limit. Consider a point: 'although differing in kind from the ordered members of a series of ever shorter lines, it is that towards which the series points. Similarly, too, in regard to a line, since it differs in kind from the ordered members of a series of ever narrower surfaces, but is that towards which the series points. A point, then, is a limit case of a line, and a line is a limit case of a surface. What would be an example of a limit, as distinct from a limit case? The upper limit of the speed of moving bodies is the speed of light'. And 'although we might be inclined to think that their speed has also a lower limit (0km/s), we should be wrong, for it is merely a limit case. Indeed, there is no lower limit simpliciter, since there is no speed below which there could not be a still lower speed. An obvious difference between the lower limit case and the upper limit simpliciter of the speed of moving bodies, therefore, is that the upper limit is indeed a speed [3.00 X 10 to the power of 8 m/s] whereas the lower limit case is not a speed at all'.[23] Since 'limit case' is an alienans adjective, a limit case speed is not a speed at all.

What, now, is a limit case instance of existence? According to Miller, instances of existence can be ordered in a decreasing order of boundedness, with an amoeba's instance of existence having more boundedness than a gazelle's, or a human being's. A limit case instance of existence is that towards which this ordered series of instances of existence points, and this is a totally unbound instance of existence, called by Miller a zero bound instance of existence.

The difficulty is to see how an ordered series of instances of existence, in which the instances of existence are less and less bounded, points towards a limit case or zero bounded instance of existence. We can see how the ordered series of ever shorter lines points to a point, and hence that there is a limit case instance of a line, because we already understand what a point is, and can see that it is that to which an ordered series of ever shorter lines points. We can see how the ordered series of ever diminishing speeds points to zero speed, and hence that there is a limit case speed, because we already understand what it is for something to be moving at zero speed: for something to be moving at zero speed is for it not to be moving at all. The following ordered series of regular polygons points to a circle: regular polygon with sides turning by 360/3 degrees at its vertices, one with sides turning by 360/4 degrees, one with sides turning by 360/5 degrees, …one with sides turning by 360/n degrees. We can see this because we already understand the notion of a circle. But we have no antecedent conception of a totally unbounded instance of existence, and so cannot see how the ordered series of less and less bounded instances of existence points to a totally unbounded instance of existence. This being so, we cannot understand Miller's doctrine that the limit case bound of existence = the limit case instance of existence. And if we cannot understand this doctrine, then we cannot understand his explanation of the notion of a Subsistent Being, and must be doubtful about whether any E=E entity exists.

Notes

1 Selves are substances, and if we hold that only events are causes, we can take this definition as short for 'a transcendent self is one an event in which causes the existence of any nonabstract nonselves there may be, etc.'
2 Hume (1955), *Dialogues*, 190–1

3 Pruss (2009), 83
4 Swinburne (1993), p. 214
5 Van Fraassen (1980), 20–21
6 Van Fraassen (1985), 255. On empirical adequacy, see Van Fraassen (1980), chs. 1–4
7 Wittgenstein (1953), I, section 281, my italics
8 See, for example, Kenny (2006), 52–3
9 Swinburne (2019), 170
10 Swinburne (2019), 169
11 Swinburne (2005), 303
12 Crean (2008), 40
13 Duns Scotus (1962), *Philosophical Writings*, 40–1
14 Feser (2014), 149
15 Miller (1992; 1996). For an excellent commentary, see Kremer (2014)
16 Kremer (2014), 64
17 Kremer (2014), 62
18 Miller (1992), 126
19 Miller (2002), 82
20 Miller (2002), 99
21 Maurin (2002), 164–6
22 Miller (1996), 66
23 Miller (1996), 7–8

4   IF SELVES DID NOT EXIST

Selves, as I defined them, are enduring substances of which this is true: for each there is a quality, which is its constant possession, which it does not share with any other substance, and which, if not remembered by it as its own, still has an affinity with a quality which some self remembers having had. I have maintained that selves, as so defined, exist. There is at least one transcendent self, at least one self that causes both the existence of any substantial nonselves there may be which are not composed of selves, and the existence of all those selves which do not cause the existence of every other self. And there is a multitude of human selves, non-transcendent, at least sometimes embodied and at least sometimes free. A self is ulterior if it is a component of a material object, defined as a concrete and substantial nonself, of which no component is a transcendent self. No sound argument has suggested itself for the doctrine that some ulterior self exists. In this final chapter, I consider the question: How would things be for us if selves as I defined them did not exist? Would things be as good as or would they be worse than actually they are? I suggest that they might well be worse. I do not suggest this with an eye to some additional and purely pragmatic argument for the positive conclusions of the earlier chapters, but rather to counter discontent with what these conclusions say is true.

Absent selves, various other entities would still exist, and some of these other entities, not selves as I define selfhood, are ones called selves by philosophers who identify them with us. Absent selves, there would still be brains and bodies and what brains and bodies constitute. There would still be causally or mnemonically united sequences of mental events, hylemorphic structures, systems of capacities for conscious stream-like experience, conscious subjects. In some sense of 'person', persons might still exist. 'I' might still refer.[1] How, then, absent selves, might things be worse?

As things are, there is an explanation both for the existence of human selves, and for the existence of substantial nonselves, if such entities exist. The explanation postulates action by at least one transcendent self. Absent selves, there would be no such action. And it is hard to see how, absent such action, the existence of substantial nonselves could be explained. If there

DOI: 10.4324/9781003274483-5

are substantial nonselves, and, absent selves they would still exist, a bleak brute fact would confront us which does not confront us as things are.

But leave that aside. How else might things be worse if selves did not exist? They would be worse if, absent selves, we were the minimal conscious subjects called selves by Strawson, or were organisms to whose existence such minimal subjects were essential. Strawson's minimal subjects have an existence which lasts no longer than the specious present or 'lived-present-of-experience', whose duration, he thinks, is no more than half a second.[2] A critic of Strawson's theory remarks that he for one has never met a sane person who seriously thought that they (sic) would cease to exist once the current experience ends. 'Thinking in this sort of way' would, he adds, 'be singularly useless for us. Our lives require complex forward planning, coupled with retrospective understanding (think here of building a cathedral, or fighting the Second World War, or writing a book), to which the idea that we endure over time, and through sleep and periods of unconsciousness, and certainly beyond the length of this experience (whatever that is) is quite indispensable'.[3] It could not be better put.

But let that too be left aside, together with the loss of the immeasurable richness of the *Kranz* of our disseveral qualities. Now to be considered is the fact that if you are a self, then for all you know you never die. This ignorance may foster hope. Suppose then that selves do not exist. Could you in that case never die? Could you exist forever if you were, not a self, but, as some philosophers think you really are, a brain or body, or composed of a brain as a statue may be composed of a lump of bronze, or a matter-form composite, the form a soul, the matter a brain or body, or a cerebrally located system of capacities for conscious stream-like experience, or a causally or mnemonically united sequence of mental events each owned by some brain or body?

Suppose that if selves did not exist, we would be brains or bodies. Might these brains or bodies be composed of ulterior selves? In Chapter 2, I looked for and failed to find a sound argument for the existence of ulterior selves. But they may for all that still exist. And if they do exist, then perhaps, for all we know, they never end, and then neither, perhaps, do the brains or bodies that they compose. What appears to be the decay and dissolution or even total annihilation of a brain or body might in that case be just the re-alignment of the hidden, never-ending ulterior selves of which it is composed. The resurrection of a body might be a restoration or even radical improvement of the original alignment, causing a new or even glorious appearance. But if selves did not exist, then neither would ulterior selves. Could you never end if you were a brain or body which was not composed of ulterior selves? Only if your body after it had died was resurrected. But if the resurrection of a body means that this very same body comes to life again, and not just that it is replaced by a duplicate, then it does not seem that, absent never-ending ulterior selves, the resurrection of a body is even possible. For a body not composed of never-ending ulterior selves may be totally annihilated, and it seems that what thus ceases to exist cannot be identical to anything that later does exist. Nor, absent never-ending ulterior selves to compose our bodies, could we live forever if we were not just brains or bodies but rather entities that brains or bodies constitute. Nor, absent never-ending ulterior selves to compose one's body, could one live forever as a matter-form composite, the form a soul, the matter a body. It may be objected that absent selves one could live forever as a matter-form composite if, as in Thomistic hylemorphism, the matter is not something composed of selves but rather prime matter which exists only in potentiality and is configured into a body by the substantial form, the soul. But to this there are two replies. The first is that in the Thomistic theory, the soul is supposed to be a conscious particular as well as what configures matter, and it is far from clear that this conscious particular is not a self, and so something that would not exist absent selves. The second reply is that *pace* Aristotle there is no such thing as something that exists only in potentiality, so that nothing that we might be, absent selves, is prime matter configured by substantial form.

If selves did not exist, there would still be sequences of mental events, and, as I assume, these mental events would not be reducible to events in brains or bodies not composed of selves. Either each mental event in such a sequence would be owned by a brain or body not composed of selves, or no event in such a sequence would have any owner other than the whole sequence of which it was a member. Either way, the sequences would for all we know be endless, and so if, absent selves, we were such sequences, there would be room for the hope that we are endless, as much room as there is for this hope if we are selves. You may wonder how, if selves did not exist, and there were mental sequences composed of events with owners other than the sequences to which they belong, these mental sequences could possibly go on forever. The owners could only be brains of bodies, and brains or bodies can go on forever only if they are composed of ulterior selves, which they would not be if no selves exist. The answer is that each mental event in the sequence might be owned by a different brain or body, in no case one composed of ulterior selves, and the sequence of these different owners might not ever end.

Let me then consider more closely how things might be for us if selves did not exist and we were infinite mental sequences. The philosophers who deny that selves exist and affirm that we are mental sequences include Derek Parfit, author of the familiar slogan 'identity is not what matters in survival'. The slogan may suggest that if selves did not exist, there would still be survival and that even if there would not then be identity, things would be as good as actually they are. But the slogan is of course ambiguous. Suppose that a person is, not a self, but a sequence of mental events. Each mental event in the sequence will then be a stage of the person which is the sequence. A self cannot be identical to both of two different selves, and a person stage cannot be identical to both of two different person stages. But if the unifying relation between the events in the sequence allows the sequence to branch, then a person stage can belong to both of two different sequences united by the same relation, and so a person stage can have two different survivors. If it is valuable that there should be sequences so unified, then it is better there should be at least some such sequences as a member of which a person stage can survive, than that, what is impossible, a person stage is identical to both of two different person stages. But this does not show if selves did not exist and we were mental sequences, then even if the sequences were infinite things would be as good as actually they are.

If selves did not exist and we were mental sequences, then our relations to the past and to other persons would in fact be quite different from, and less valuable than, the relations which selves can have to what they have done and to other selves. A self can come to terms with or be forgiven for what it once did. And a self can love another self without thereby loving its own self. The same possibilities are not open for a person who is not a self but a mental sequence.

A sequence of mental events does not exist at a time but rather elapses over time. So if you were an infinite mental sequence, then there would be no time in the past at which you did anything, let alone anything with which you could come to terms or for which you could be forgiven. A sequence of mental events can be loved, but it can love another mental sequence only in the etiolated sense that it has as a member an event of loving that other mental sequence, and a mental sequence can love another mental sequence without thereby loving itself only in the etiolated sense that it has as a member a mental event which, though an event of loving that other mental sequence, is not an event which is a member of that other sequence. Suppose a person is an infinite mental sequence in which each event bears some relation R to the next member: suppose, as we might put it, that a person is an R-based infinite mental sequence. Any R-based mental sequence S has another R-based mental sequence S' as a proper part. So no member of S' can love the whole of S without thereby loving a mental event which is also a member of and so part of S'. So even in the etiolated sense, S' cannot love the whole of S without loving itself. A figure will make this plain (Figure 4.1).

Here the stars represent mental events, and that a line joins two stars represents the fact that the mental event represented by the first star bears the relation R to the mental event represented by the second star. Let X be

Figure 4.1

84 If Selves Did Not Exist

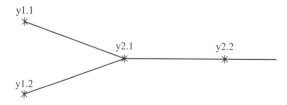

Figure 4.2

the R-based sequence of mental events which begins with x1 and includes x2 and x3. Let X' be the R-based sequence of mental events which begins with x2 and includes x3. Since X' is a proper part of X, no member of X' can be an event of loving all the members of X without being an event of loving itself.

It may seem that the difficulty can be avoided if we say that, absent selves, we might be maximal infinite mental sequences, in the sense of infinite mental sequences which are not parts of other mental sequences. Then, absent selves, X might be a person even if X' is not. But it seems that there is no such thing as a maximal infinite sequence: for any infinite sequence, there is another infinite sequence of which it is a part.

Nor is what have I been describing the only way in which a mental sequence cannot love another mental sequence without thereby loving itself. Figure 4.1 illustrates a difficulty that arises whatever the relation is between the events in a mental sequence. But the same difficulty arises in a different way when the relation between the events in a mental sequence is the kind of relation most often postulated by those who, denying that selves exist, think that we are mental sequences. Let an R-based mental sequence now be one made up of mental events each of which is either causally related to or psychologically continuous with the next member. In Figures 4.2 and 4.3, each star represents a mental event, and that a line joins two stars represents the fact that the mental event represented by the first star is R-related to the mental event represented by the second star.

Consider Figure 4.2. Let Y1 be the R-based sequence of mental events which begins with y1.1 and includes both y2.1 and y 2. 2, and let Y2 be

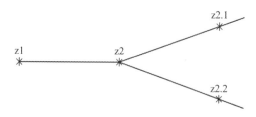

Figure 4.3

the R-based sequence of mental events which begins with y1.2 and includes both y2.1 and y2.2. Since Y2 has some members which are also members of Y1, it has some members which cannot be events of loving all the members of Y1 without also being events of loving themselves. Next, consider Figure 4.3.

Let Z1 be the R-based mental sequence containing z1, z2 and z2.1, and let Z2 be the R-based mental sequence containing z1, z2, and z2.2. Since Z2 has some members which are also members of Z1, it has some members which cannot be events of loving all the members of Z1 without also being events of loving themselves.

Can there be mental sequences which do not overlap in the way that Y2 overlaps Y1 and Z2 overlaps Z1? And might it not be that if selves did not exist, we would be such non-overlapping mental sequences? That is certainly a logical possibility. There could be an infinite mental sequence in which each mental event was related to the next mental event by virtue of sharing with it quality which it did not share with any other simultaneous mental event. Even if selves did not exist, there could be many such non-overlapping mental sequences, as many of them as there are, in actuality, different selves. Timothy Sprigge seems to have proposed that such non-overlapping mental sequences are what we are. He wrote that in early infancy 'an individual style of experiencing the world is established which will be present all along the series of moments of consciousness constituting my subsequent conscious life and can be called my personal essence...The thing which is the same is not some thin abstraction, such as a numerically identical pure ego which could survive all changes of character, but rather a (more or less) distinctive style of feeling the world handed on from moment to moment in the stream of consciousness which remains generically the same though in different specific versions'.[4] It is not entirely easy to imagine what these distinctive styles of feeling might be. They would, I suppose, be qualities of the mental events which make up each mental sequence. But it is hard to imagine what might cause all the contents of the events in a given mental sequence to have a single constant quality if this was not some feature of the subject or subjects of the events in the sequence. If the subject were a single self, we could suppose that its disseveral quality somehow tinged in a uniform way all the contents of the events in the sequence. But, we are supposing, selves do not exist, so the subject must be a single brain or body not composed of selves. If it is a single brain or body not composed of selves which is the subject of all the events in the sequence, then the limited lifespan of the subject will be incompatible with the endlessness of the sequence. But if the events in the sequence belong to a succession of different brains or bodies not composed of selves, then we are left without an explanation of the uniform quality of the contents of the events in the sequence. And whatever the quality common to all the events in a given mental sequence, that sequence will still have as a proper part another mental sequence, the events in which will share the same quality. If these mental sequences were both persons, then the second would be unable to love the first without thereby loving itself. Fortunately, selves are not like that.

Notes

1 For details of some doctrines called theories of selfhood but on my definitions self-denying, see Heil (2013), Olson (2007), Noonan (2013), Jaworski (2016), Dainton (2008; 2014), and Strawson (2009a; 2009b)
2 Strawson (2009a), 252
3 Snowdon (2018)
4 Sprigge (1988), 48

EXCURSUS

A: Primitive Modality

In the discussion of our freedom in section 1.8, I affirmed that sometimes one has an experience of being both able in one's present circumstances to decide to A, and able in one's present circumstances, to decide not to A. I maintained that neither ability is analysable. Each is a primitive modality. And because these abilities are experienced, their ascription to selves is meaningful even on the stringent conditions for being meaningful laid down by the attractive and developed form of Hume's concept empiricism known as Empirical Atomism. I have been sceptical, however, about the existence of any other primitive modalities. On causality and laws of nature, I have eschewed natural necessity and taken a Humean, indeed Quinean, line.[1] Counterfactuals I have regarded as open to demystification, by way of reduction to contingent propositions purely about the actual world. For 'possible' as it figures in the independence condition for substantiality, I have offered a psychological analysis. I have been sceptical about the existence of primitive causal powers. Some of the things that I have said about selfhood may perfectly well still stand even if I am wrong about the non-existence of primitive modalities which are not experienced human abilities. But I am far from sure that if I were wrong about that, then I could continue to maintain that there is at least one transcendent self. The argument in Chapter 3 for the existence of at least one transcendent self was an argument for the existence of at least one self which causes all the beta entities to exist, where a beta entity is defined as a non-abstract entity which is either a non-transcendent self or a nonself, no component of which is a transcendent self. But in section 3.6, we encountered a regress argument, of scholastic provenance, for the existence of an E=E entity, for the existence of an entity whose essence is its existence. Suppose that this regress argument is sound. Then the question arises of whether an E=E entity is a beta entity. It cannot be, if there is a transcendent self which causes all the beta entities to exist, for an E=E entity can hardly be caused to exist by something else. So either an E=E entity is itself a transcendent self, or there is a fault in the Chapter 3 argument for the existence of at least one transcendent self. But, so it seems, an E=E entity cannot be a self of any kind. How can it be a self if the essence of an E=E entity is its existence, and the essence of a self is its disseveral quality? Should we then try to preserve the Chapter 3 argument for the existence of at least one transcendent self by denying the soundness of the regress argument for the existence of an E=E entity? The regress argument employs the notion of a causal power, and it will be sound only if 'power' in 'causal power' is meaningful. If it is indeed meaningful, then its meaning either will or will not be analysable in non-modal terms. There seems not to be any non-modal analysis of its meaning which will help us to uphold the soundness of the regress argument. Is it, then, a meaningful but primitive modal term? Not if, as I suggested in section 1.6, the only primitive modal terms made meaningful by our experience are those which denote the ability of a self to will. I need then to defend that restriction if I am to preserve the Chapter 3 argument for the existence of at least one transcendent self.

According to Richard Swinburne, we have experiences of exerting causal influence on our own bodies, experiences which are not just of being able to will or to make decisions. And Swinburne maintains that thanks to these experiences of exerting causal influence on our own bodies, we do indeed have intelligible and primitive concepts of causal power and natural necessitation. 'We are ourselves aware of causing effects, by exerting causal influence which– given the right physical conditions – makes it naturally necessary that they will occur. The innumerable paradigm examples of such intentional causation make the concept of natural necessity intelligible, and so even on Hume's theory of concept empiricism it is a coherent concept'.[2] According to Hume, the will 'has no more a discoverable connection with its effects than any material cause has with its proper effect'; such a connection 'could not be foreseen without the experience of their constant conjunction'. Against this, Swinburne claims that 'I could not even identify a volition as mine as I perform it without thinking of it as causally influential'. I do not agree. Can I not perfectly well will the orange to stop rolling before it reaches the edge of the table and identify this volition as my own without being superstitious enough to believe that my volition will really make it stop? But even if we do have experiences of exercising causal influence on our own bodies, there is no good reason to take the anthropomorphic step of supposing that seemingly inanimate events exercise something analogous to that sort of influence on each other. Swinburne believes that unless we suppose that laws of nature describe ways in which inanimate events exert a causal influence on each other which is analogous to the influence which he thinks we exert on our own bodies, we will have to take it that laws of nature describe just contingent regularities, and accept that whether a particular event ε causes another particular event γ now depends not merely on what has happened but on what will happen in the whole future history of the universe. We will have to take it that whether ε causes γ may depend on what happens in two billion years time, and so if the world ends before then, certain events which otherwise would happen (e.g., that some event like ε is not followed by an event like γ) will not happen, which may make a difference to whether it is the case now that ε causes γ. This, Swinburne maintains, goes against the normal understanding implicit in paradigm examples of one event causing another, on which what makes it the case that ε now causes γ and explains why γ occurs issome state of the world now. On this normal understanding, what is yet to happen in two billion years' time can make no difference to what is the true explanation of why γ occurs. Why though, I ask, should the fact, if it is a fact, that we ordinarily suppose that inanimate events exert a causal influence on each other entitle us to make the anthropomorphic supposition that they really do? It is not as if no alternatives are available to what we ordinarily suppose. We could, for example, adopt David Lewis's proposal that while one event causes another only if a law of nature links the two events, laws of nature are theorems in the best systematisations of all contingent facts.[3] Nor will it do to say that unless we accept that there are primitive natural necessities, we will not have that knowledge of Induction's reliability which we obviously do possess, and cannot do without. For, as I will suggest when in the next Excursus I come on to consensual propositions, we may not on reflection even *want* to have such knowledge.

Nobody will deny that there are modal terms which are in some contexts used with a meaning which can be captured in entirely non-modal terms. There are, for example, contexts in which 'it could be that p' means merely 'I do not know that not-p' or in which 'It can A' means no more than something of the form 'It will A if —'. The more such non-modal analyses we can identify, the less startlingly radical may the doctrine seem that, outside our abilities to make decisions, there are no meaningful primitive modalities. Let me try, then, to identify a few.

(1) Perhaps, by the substitution of synonyms for synonyms, some modal sentences can be reduced to non-modal sentences which express logical truths. So, for example, in 'Necessarily all bachelors are unmarried', the seemingly primitive modality of 'necessarily' may in this way be made to evaporate. 'Necessarily all bachelors are unmarried' is reduced to 'Unmarried men are unmarried', which expresses a logical truth in the sense that it would continue to express a truth whatever substitutions were made for its non-logical terms.

(2) The distinction may be wielded between sentences and statements. Consider 'The number which is the number of the planets is necessarily greater than 6'. This may be taken to mean that in a context where 'the number of the planets' refers to the number 9, the sentence 'The number which is the number of the planets is greater than 6' expresses a statement whose negation is a contradiction, namely that 9 is not greater than 6. Similarly, 'Hesperus is necessarily Phosphorus' may be supposed to mean that in a context where 'Hesperus' and 'Phosphorus' refer to

the same individual, the sentence 'Hesperus is Phosphorus' expresses a statement whose negation is a contradiction, namely the statement expressed by 'Hesperus is Hesperus'. The distinction between a sentence and a statement can be explained as follows. 'The statement which a token sentence *s* expresses is that element of claim in what is said which is made by any other token sentence *r* which predicates the same properties of the same individuals, at the same times and places (however the individuals, times and places are picked out), when properties are the same if and only if the predicates which designate them are synonymous. So two sentences express the same statement if and only if they attribute the same property to the same individuals at the same place and time, whatever the way of referring (or "mode of presentation"...) by which those individuals, places and times are picked out'. Statements are also to be distinguished from propositions. 'The proposition which a token sentence *s* expresses is that element of claim in what is said which is also made by any other token sentence...which is synonymous with *s*. Two sentences express the same proposition if and only if they are synonymous. "Rex mortuus est" uttered by a Latin speaker of the fourteenth century, "Le roi est mort" uttered by a French speaker of the eighteenth century, and "The king is dead" uttered by an English speaker of the twentieth century express the same proposition. ... The three token sentences just cited did not express the same statement, for (we may reasonably suppose) they concern different kings. Whereas, "I am ill", spoken by me, "You are ill", addressed to me, and "He is ill", spoken of me, all spoken at the same time, do all express the same statement (although not the same proposition)'.[4]

(3) The speculation may be deployed that there exists a plurality of concrete but spatio-temporally and causally unrelated worlds of which our own actual world is but one. With this assumed, 'Necessarily everything is either F or G' comes out as the non-modal 'In no world is there something which is both F and G'. Sentences of the form 'a is necessarily F' also come out as non-modal if the theory of a plurality of worlds is supplemented by a theory of counterparts, which would make the sentence equivalent to one about the existence and F-ness, in at least one other world, of something more similar to a than anything else in that world.

(4) It may be assumed that God exists, and sentences of the form 'possibly p' and 'necessarily p' may then be taken as equivalent to sentences about God's nature or about what God thinks or wills. It may be said that 'the being of necessary truths consists in their being recognised or accepted as true by God, though the reason why they are true (and hence accepted) rather than false (and hence rejected) is to be found in their content rather than in the divine acceptance as such'.[5]

(5) It may be proposed that every sentence of the form 'necessarily p' is equivalent to a sentence of the form '(i) p, and (ii) not-p is unintelligible', in which the modal 'unintelligible' is in turn non-modally analysed. To

get that last analysis, we take 'q is unintelligible' to be equivalent to a conditional, which is further analysed in terms of a de facto regularity. The conditional will be 'were anyone to try to understand q then they would fail', which is in turn taken as a condensed argument, one premise of which is the generalisation 'Everyone who tries to understand q fails'. Thus, 'Necessarily nothing is red and green all over at the same time' is supposed to be equivalent to '(i) nothing is red and green all over at the same time' and (ii) everyone who tries to understand the negation of (i) fails. And 'Necessarily no proposition is both true and false' is equivalent to '(i) no proposition is both true and false, and (ii) everyone who tries to understand the negation of (i) fails'.[6]

(6) It may be proposed that every sentence of the form 'necessarily p' is equivalent to a sentence of the form '(i) p is true, and (ii) that p belongs to a class of truths C' where C is non-modally defined in terms of p's content. Thus 'Necessarily no proposition is both true and false' is equivalent to '(i) no proposition is both true and false, and (ii) that no proposition is both true and false belongs to the class of logical truths. And 'Necessarily parthood is transitive' is equivalent to 'parthood is transitive' and (ii) that parthood is transitive belongs to the class of metaphysical truths.[7]

I did not claim in Chapter 3 that transcendent selves are necessary beings, and you may indeed wonder whether there is any way to count 'necessary being' as meaningful, given the restrictions I have envisaged on the meaningfulness of primitive modal terms. If we exclude the pluriversal and theological analyses of 'necessary being', we are left with three would-be alternatives: (i) 'x is a necessary being' means (a) x exists, and (b) 'x does not exist' is contradictory; (ii) 'x is a necessary being' means (a) x exists, and (c) everyone who tries to understand 'x does not exist' fails; and (iii) 'x is a necessary being means' (a) x exists, and (d) 'x exists' belongs to some such non-modally defined class of truths as the class of logical truths or the class of metaphysical truths. If x is a concrete individual, as distinct from an abstract entity such as a property or number, then neither (i) nor (ii) seems to work. We do not know of any property F such that 'if x is F, then x does not exist' is contradictory or such that if x is F, then everyone who tries to understand 'x does not exist' fails. What of (iii)? The non-modally defined class of truths would presumably be the class of metaphysical truths. But if 'x exists' belongs to the class of metaphysical truths, it does so regardless of whether 'x exists' is necessary or contingent. The classificatory analysis likewise will not serve.

B: Consensual Propositions

When arguing in Chapter 3 for the existence of at least one transcendent self, I relied on two explanatory principles. The second of these two principles was Evidential Sufficient Reason, which says that there is a causal explanation for p's truth if and only if there is no strong and undefeated evidence that there is no such explanation. In section 3.2, I provided two arguments for the truth of this principle. The second and by far the simpler of these two arguments was inductive, and the complaint was imagined that the reliability of induction is something of which we have no knowledge. My reply is to suggest that it is a *consensual* proposition that Induction is reliable, and that if a proposition is consensual and you believe that proposition, then you may not on reflection even *want* to know that it is true.[8]

A proposition is consensual if and only if (i) almost anyone who entertains it firmly believes it; (ii) almost anyone who entertains (i) firmly believes (i); (iii) almost anyone who entertains (ii) firmly believes (ii); and so on, ad infinitum. That Induction is reliable is, I think, consensual. So is the proposition that we are many. Though I have affirmed with some confidence that we exist for longer than it takes to have an experience, that proposition is, I fear, not consensual. There are Buddhists who regard it as a dangerous falsehood.

What then is the connection between believing a consensual proposition and not wanting to know that it is true? To answer this question, we must ask what makes knowledge preferable to true belief. To that one stock answer comes from Plato's *Meno*: knowledge less likely to 'run away'.[9] When true belief comes under pressure, it is less likely to disintegrate if it is also knowledge. If it is knowledge, then there is evidence to prop it up, or at least there is a chance that the reliable process can be repeated by means of which the belief was first generated. Another stock answer concerns the public good. When your own true belief is also knowledge, this increases the chances that others will grasp the truth that you believe. Your evidence is perhaps publicly available: others can get hold of it too. The reliable process by which your belief was first acquired can also do its work for others. It may even be that you will be able to function as a source of information about the truth-value of what you know: you have a property, detectable to persons to whom it is not yet detectable that p, which correlates in a lawlike, non-accidental way with your being right that p.[10]

Suppose now that N wants to know that P but thinks that he has no such knowledge. If P is consensual, then by (i) he is likely to believe that P, and by (ii) he is likely to believe that (a) almost anyone who entertains P will firmly believe it. And if he believes that (a) then he is likely to infer that (b) it is likely that he will believe P whenever he entertains that proposition. But if all this is right, then he is likely to think that the two stock reasons for wanting knowledge do not apply to his knowing that P. If he believes that (b) he will think that the 'running away' reason does not apply. If he believes that (a) he will think that if he knew that P, this would do nothing to increase the chances that others would come to believe that P. He will think that to believe that P, these others need only entertain the proposition. They will not need the evidence or generally reliable process of belief formation by virtue of which he would know that P. They will not need him as a source of information.

Don't we on reflection want any knowledge just for its own sake, even knowledge of consensual propositions? That seems doubtful. It is much more likely that when you do indeed want knowledge, you want it for the sake of true belief, either your own true belief (as in the running away story), or the true belief of others (as in the other stock story). Even if it is true that ten thousand years ago an ant was standing just where my foot is now, I do not mind not knowing that it was. In the rhetoric of the academy, things are of course otherwise: it is for its own sake that we are to value knowledge. But whenever in such contexts 'knowledge' does not function just as an imposing stand-in for true belief, the real thought seems to be that there is an intrinsic value in the intellectual virtue which is required for the pursuit of knowledge, or in the formal beauty of certain organised bodies of true propositions whose organisation is contingent on their evidential relations.

I have suggested that if P is consensual, then N will be saved from wanting to know that P by believing the three propositions, P, (a) almost anyone who entertains P will firmly believe it, and (b) it is likely that he will believe P whenever he entertains that proposition. May he not wonder whether these saving beliefs of his are really true? I suggest that if he does indeed have these beliefs, and does raise this question, then his answer to the question can only be 'Yes, they are true'. Let S be the conjunction of the three propositions, and suppose that he believes that S. His belief that S is either dispositional or occurrent, and if occurrent, then it will cause him to have a dispositional belief that S. But a dispositional belief that p is in part a disposition to say 'Yes' in answer to the self-addressed question 'Is p true?'. And by the same token, if he does indeed believe that S, and also believes that he believes that S, then 'Yes it is' will be his answer to the self-addressed question, 'Is my belief that S true?'. A dispositional belief that you believe that p is in part a disposition to answer 'Yes' to the self-addressed question, 'Do I believe that p?'. Put a dispositional belief that p together with a dispositional belief that you believe that p, and ask yourself the question 'Is my belief that p true?' and then by the very nature of the two dispositions, your answer will be 'Yes it is'. Maybe you can stifle that answer, by somehow treating yourself as if you were someone else, like Sartre's girl who when the man takes her hand tries to observe the event as if it isn't really happening to *her* at all, as if the hand he has taken is not really her own hand which she can herself decide brusquely to snatch away, but an alien object whose movements she cannot control. If however you have a properly existential attitude to your own attitudes, then 'Yes it is' will be the answer that emerges.

At this point, someone will say that really N *should* stand back and view his own beliefs in a more objective way. Suppose he believes that S, and believes he believes it. Then *I* won't be surprised, if *he* answers 'Yes it is' when he asks himself whether he has a true belief that S. But there is nothing here which guarantees that *I* believe that S, and nothing therefore which prevents *me* from believing that if he did know that S, then his belief would be more likely to be true. Shouldn't he then be prepared to put himself in *my* place, when considering whether S is true? Shouldn't he be prepared to look at things in a way which would be equally acceptable to me? These

94 *Excursus*

scruples are inapplicable in the case of a consensual proposition. If P is consensual, I too will believe that S if I entertain it.

But what about 'I believe that p but of course I may be wrong.'? This kind of remark is often made, with seeming sincerity, even by people who do both believe that p and believe that they believe it. But does it not follow from the line I have taken that if you do believe that p, you are disposed to believe that you are *definitely right*? A.M. McIver once set an *Analysis* competition in which the task was to explain how such remarks are to be taken. As he reported, the problem had no solvers and in fact there were only two competitors. Attempting his own solution, McIver suggested that when I say 'I am aware that I may be wrong', I may perhaps just be saying in an oddly misleading way that, even if I have no doubt that I am right, yet, *if* something were to happen which I must think will *not* happen (namely, that I should be proved wrong), *then* I should alter my opinion'. But he was not happy with this solution: '...what is required is not only that I should *declare myself* disposed to change my mind for good reason, but that I should actually *be* (or at least *think myself*) so disposed, and it is a fact of experience that to *be* so disposed, if it is possible at all, requires continuous effort and resistance to temptation; but why should I ever make this effort unless I recognise that, if I do not, then I am in danger of being left with opinions which are false? But this seems to bring us right back to our original difficulty, because it seems to imply that I must recognise that my present opinions *perhaps are* false'.[11] If I had entered McIver's competition, I think I would have said just that 'I believe that p but I am aware that I may be wrong' is a piece of innocent diplomatic insincerity. (Cf. Wittgenstein: '"x is in error" has no real point for x= myself'[12], and 'If there were a verb meaning "to believe falsely", it would not have a significant first person present indicative'.[13])

A final worry. What if the proposition not known to be true is that P is consensual? A proposition is consensual if and only if (i) almost anyone who entertains it firmly believes it; (ii) almost anyone who entertains (i) firmly believes (i); (iii) almost anyone who entertains (ii) firmly believes (ii); and so on, ad infinitum. By this definition, 'p is consensual' is itself consensual. This is because each conjunct i of the infinite conjunction which is equivalent to 'p is consensual' will itself be the first conjunct of an infinite conjunction which is equivalent to 'i is consensual'. Thus (i) is the first member of an infinite conjunction whose next conjunct is (ii) and which is equivalent to '(i) is consensual', (ii) is the first conjunct of an infinite conjunction whose next conjunct is (iii) and which is equivalent to '(ii) is consensual, and so on.

Notes

1 'I see no higher or more austere necessity than natural necessity; and in natural necessity, or our attributions of it I see only Hume's regularities, culminating here or there in what passes for an explanatory trait or the promise of it' [Quine (1966), 56]. Some writers have in recent years laboured to show that in point of fact, Hume was not after all the great denier of necessary con-

nections. If they are right, then as David Lewis remarked in reply to one such writer, nothing much follows except that in 'Humean theory of causality', 'Humean' should be replaced by "Humean" and a footnote.
2. Swinburne (2013), 128
3. Lewis (1973), 73–4; Beebee (2000)
4. Swinburne (1994), 98. A qualification. 'For a statement to be necessary, the sentence that expresses the negation of that statement and that expresses a statement that entails a contradiction, must pick out the individuals, times and places involved by rigid designators'. A rigid designator is an expression that picks out the individual that it does quite independently of whether that individual gains or loses essential properties. This 'this red lectern' is not a rigid designator because it picks out a lectern only while that lectern has the non-essential property of being red. 'Without this qualification all sentences would turn out to express necessary statements! "This lectern is red" clearly does not express a necessary statement. But it expresses the same statement as "This red lectern is red" and the negation of that sentence expresses a proposition that entails a self-contradiction...Rigid designators include proper names (e.g., Hesperus) and descriptions of individuals in terms of their essential properties. The essential properties of material objects include the essential kinds to which they belong and the matter of which they are made. So "lectern made of chunk of wood W" (where W is the name of a chunk of wood) is a rigid designator' (ibid., 103)
5. A doctrine to which, according to Robert Adams [(1994), 191], Leibniz should have been led. For a full and rigorous development of this idea, see Leftow (2012)
6. One writer who seems somewhat shyly to favour the idea that 'Necessarily p' is equivalent to a sentence of the form '(i) p, and (ii) not-p is unintelligible' is Simon Blackburn. There is, he thinks, a class of propositions 'of whose truth we can make nothing' [Blackburn (1993), 70]. We can make something of a way of thought in which it is not realised that there are trees. We cannot make anything of the thought that 1+1 does not equal 2. Should we infer from our inability to make anything of the truth of some proposition that this proposition is absolutely impossible? Blackburn believes that there is a quite proper move or inference here. And in fact he is 'sceptical about the assumption that we know what we mean by...the real distribution of possibilities, in a way that allows us to contrast them wholesale with the blocks that our only ways of thinking meet'. (ibid., 67)
7. See Sider (2003), 202–5
8. I draw in the rest of this Excursus on ch. 1 of my (2001)
9. 'True opinions are a fine thing and do all sorts of good so long as they stay in their place, but they will not stay long. They run away from a man's mind; so they are not worth much until you tether them by working out the reason'. (Plato, *Meno*, 97d–98a)
10. Craig (1990), 18, 25
11. McIver (1956), 29–30
12. Wittgenstein (1982), remark no. 427
13. Wittgenstein (1953), 190

REFERENCES

Adams, R. 1994. *Leibniz*, New York: Oxford University Press.
Armstrong, D. 1968. *A Materialist Theory of the Mind*, London: Routledge.
Ayer, A.J. 1959. 'Freedom and Necessity', in *Philosophical Essays*, London: MacMillan.
Balaguer, M. 2010. *Free Will as an Open Scientific Problem*, Cambridge, Mass: The MIT Press.
Bayne, T. 2010. *The Unity of Consciousness*, Oxford: Oxford University Press.
Beebee, H. 2000. 'The Non-Governing Conception of Laws of Nature', *Philosophy and Phenomenological Research*, 61, 571–594.
Berkeley, (1948) 'Philosophical Commentaries', in A.A. Luce and T.E. Jessop, *The Works of George Berkeley*, Edinburgh: Nelson.
Black, M. 1952. 'The Identity of Indiscernibles', *Mind*, 61, 153–164.
Blackburn, S. 1993. 'Morals and Modals', in *Essays in Quasi-Realism*, New York: Oxford University Press.
Broackes, J. 2006. 'Substance', *Proceedings of the Aristotelian Society*, 106, 131–166.
Broad, C.D. 1933. *Examination of McTaggart's Philosophy*, vol. 1, Cambridge: Cambridge University Press.
Broad, C.D. 1952. 'Determinism, Indeterminism and Libertarianism', in *Ethics and the History of Philosophy*, London: Routledge
Broad, C.D. 1962. *Lectures on Psychical Research*, London: Routledge.
Brüntrup, G. and Jaskolla, L. (eds.) 2017. *Panpsychism: Contemporary Perspectives*, Oxford: Oxford University Press.
Chalmers, D. 2017. 'The Combination Problem for Panpsychism', in Brüntrup G. and Jaskolla, 179–214.
Corcoran, K. (ed.) 2001. *Soul, Body and Survival*, Ithaca: Cornell University Press.
Craig, E. 1990. *Knowledge and the State of Nature*, Oxford: Clarendon Press.
Crane, T. 2001. *Elements of Mind*, Oxford: Oxford University Press.
Crean, T. 2008. *A Catholic Replies to Professor Dawkins*, Oxford: Family Publications.
Dainton, B. 2008. *The Phenomenal Self*, Oxford: Oxford University Press.
Dainton, B. 2010. *Time and Space*, 2nd Edition, Durham: Acumen.
Dainton, B. 2014. *Self*, London: Penguin Books.
Dainton, B. 2016. 'The Sense of Self', *Proceedings of the Aristotelian Society Supplementary Volume*, 90, 113–143.

Descartes. 1985. *Principles of Philosophy*, in John Cottingham, Robert Stoothoff, Dugald Murdoch (tr.) *Philosophical Writings*, vol. I, Cambridge: Cambridge University Press.
Descartes. 1984. *Meditations*, in John Cottingham et al. (tr.) *Philosophical Writings*, vol. II, Cambridge: Cambridge University Press.
Feser, E. 2014. *Scholastic Metaphysics*, Heusenstamm: Editiones Scholasticae.
Foster, J. 1985. *A.J.Ayer*, London: Routledge.
Foster, J. 1991. *The Immaterial Self*, London: Routledge.
Foster, J. 2008. *A World for Us*, Oxford: Oxford University Press.
Van Fraassen, B. 1980. *The Scientific Image*, Oxford: Clarendon Press.
Van Fraassen, B. 1985. 'Empiricism in the Philosophy of Science', in P. Churchland and C. Hooker (eds.) *Images of Science*, Chicago: Chicago University Press.
Frankfurt, H. 1969. 'Alternate Possibilities and Moral Responsibility', *Journal of Philosophy*, 66, 829–839.
Geach, P. 1979. *Truth, Love and Immortality*, London: Hutchinson.
Ginet, C. 1990. *On Action*, Cambridge: Cambridge University Press.
Goetz, S. 2018. 'Against Animalism', in Loose *et al*, 307–315.
Goff, P. 2017a. *Consciousness and Fundamental Reality*, Oxford: University Press.
Goff, P. 2017b. 'Panpsychism', in *Schneider and Velmans*, 106–124.
Grunberger, R. 1974. *A Social History of the Third Reich*, Harmondsworth: Penguin Books.
Hasker, W. 2001. *The Emergent Self*, Ithaca: Cornell University Press.
Heil, J. 2013. *Philosophy of Mind*, London: Routledge.
Wong, H.Y. 2007. 'Cartesian Psychophysics', in *Van Inwagen and Zimmerman*, 169–195.
Hopkins, G.M. 1959. *Sermons and Devotional Writings*, C. Devlin (ed.), Oxford: Clarendon Press.
Hume. 1955. *Dialogues on Natural Religion*, N. Kemp Smith (ed.), London: Nelson.
Hume. 1978. *A Treatise of Human Nature*, L. Selby-Bigge (ed.), Oxford: Clarendon Press.
Van Inwagen, P. 1983. *An Essay on Free Will*, Oxford: Clarendon Press.
Van Inwagen, P. and Zimmerman, D. (eds.) 2007. *Persons, Human and Divine*, Oxford: Clarendon Press.
Jackson, F. 1977. *Perception*, Cambridge: Cambridge University Press.
Jaworski, W. 2016. *Structure and the Metaphysics of Mind*, Oxford: Oxford University Press.
Kenny, A. 2006. *What I Believe*, London: Continuum.
Kim, J. 2001. 'Lonely Souls: Causality and Substance Dualism', in K. Corcoran (ed.) *Soul, Body and Survival*, Ithaca: Cornell University Press.
Kim, J. 2018. 'Against Substance Dualism', in J. Loose *et al.*, 152–167.
Körner, S. 1966. *Experience and Theory*, London: Routledge.
Kremer, E. 2014. *Analysis of Existing*, New York: Bloomsbury.
Kriegel, U. 2015. 'For-Me-Ness', in D.O. Dahlstrom (ed.) *Philosophy of Mind and Phenomenology*, London: Routledge.
Ladyman, J. and Ross, D. 2007. *Everything Must Go*, Oxford: Oxford University Press.
Leftow, B. 2012. *God and Necessity*, Oxford: Oxford University Press.
Lewis, D. 1973. *Counterfactuals*, Oxford: Blackwell.

References

Lewis, D. 1986. *On the Plurality of Worlds*, Oxford: Blackwell.
Lewis, D. 1989. 'Dispositional Theories of Value', *Proceedings of the Aristotelian Society Supplementary Volume*, 63, 113-137.
Lloyd, A.C. 1985. 'The Self in Berkeley's Philosophy', in J. Foster and H. Robinson (eds.) *Essays on Berkeley*, Oxford: Oxford University Press.
Longuenesse, B. 2017. *I, Me, Mine*, Oxford: Oxford University Press.
Loose, J., Menuge, A. and Moreland, J.P. (eds.) 2018. *The Blackwell Companion to Substance Dualism*, Oxford: Wiley-Blackwell.
Lowe, E. 2002. *A Survey of Metaphysics*, Oxford: Oxford University Press.
Mackie, J. 1976. *Problems from Locke*, Oxford: Oxford University Press.
Mackie, P. 2006. *How Things Might Have Been*, Oxford: Clarendon Press.
McDowell, J. 1983. 'Aesthetic Value, Objectivity and the Fabric of the World', in E. Schaper (ed.), *Pleasure, Preference and Value*, Cambridge: Cambridge University Press, 1-16.
McDowell, J. 1994. *Mind and World*, Cambridge, Mass: Harvard University Press.
McIver, A. 1956. 'Report on the Problem "How can I Think It Possible That I May Be Mistaken?"', *Analysis*, 17, 25-30.
McTaggart, J. 1921, 1927. *The Nature of Existence*, Cambridge: Cambridge University Press.
Maurin, A. 2002. *If Tropes*, Dordrecht: Kluwer.
Miller, B. 1992. *From Existence to God*, London: Routledge.
Miller, B. 1996. *A Most Unlikely God*, Notre Dame: Notre Dame University Press.
Miller, B. 2002. *The Fullness of Being*, Notre Dame: Notre Dame University Press.
Nathan, N. 1986. 'Simple Colours', *Philosophy*, 61, 345-353.
Nathan, N. 1991. 'McTaggart's Immaterialism', *The Philosophical Quarterly*, 41, 442-456.
Nathan, N. 2001. *The Price of Doubt*, London: Routledge.
Noonan, H. 2013. *Personal Identity*, 3rd Edition, London: Routledge.
Olson, E. 2001. 'A Compound of Two Substances', in *Corcoran*, 73-88.
Olson, E. 2007. *What Are We?*, Oxford: Oxford University Press.
Papineau, D. 2009. 'Physical Causal Closure and Naturalism', in B. McLaughlin, A. Beckermann and S. Walter (eds.) *The Oxford Handbook of Philosophy of Mind*, Oxford: Clarendon Press.
Plato, 1956. *Meno*, Guthrie, W. (tr.), Harmondsworth: Penguin
Pruss, A. 2009. 'The Leibnizian Cosmological Argument', in W.L. Craig and J.P. Moreland (eds.) *The Blackwell Companion to Natural Theology*, Oxford: Wiley-Blackwell.
Quine, W. 1966. 'Necessary Truth', in *The Ways of Paradox*, New York: Random House.
Quine, W. 1969. 'Natural Kinds', in *Ontological Relativity and Other Essays*, New York: Columbia University Press.
Robinson, H. 2007. 'The Self and Time', in *Van Inwagen and Zimmerman*, 55-83.
Russell, B. 1912. *The Problems of Philosophy*, London: Williams and Norgate.
Russell, B. 1948. *Human Knowledge: Its Scope and Limits*, London: Allen and Unwin.
Russell, B. 1956. 'Mind and Matter', in *Portraits from Memory*. London: Allen and Unwin.
Schneider, S. and Velmans, M. (eds.) 2017. *The Blackwell Companion to Consciousness*, Oxford: Wiley-Blackwell.

References

Schopenhauer, 1976. *The World as Will and Representation*, E.J.F. Payne (tr.), New York: Dover.
Scotus, D. 1962. *Philosophical Writings*, Allan Wolter (ed. and tr.), London: Nelson.
Sider, T. 2003. 'Reductive Theories of Modality', in M. Loux and D. Zimmerman (eds.), *The Oxford Handbook of Metaphysics*, Oxford: Oxford University Press
Siderits, M., Thompson, E. and Zahavi, D. 2011. *Self, No Self?*, Oxford: Oxford University Press.
Simons, P. 1998. 'Farewell to Substance: A Differentiated Leave-taking', *Ratio*, 11, 235–251.
Snowdon, P. 2018. Review of Galen Strawson, *The Subject of Experience*, in *Notre Dame Philosophical Reviews*, 2018.04.20.
Sprigge, T. 1988. 'Personal and Impersonal Identity', *Mind*, 98, 29–49.
Stein, E. 2006. *Endliches Und Ewiges Sein*, Freiburg: Herder.
Strawson, G. 1994. 'The Impossibility of Moral Responsibility', *Philosophical Studies*, 75, 5–24.
Strawson, G. 2002. 'The Bounds of Freedom', in R. Kane (ed.) *The Oxford Handbook of Free Will*, Oxford: Oxford University Press.
Strawson, G. 2009a. *Selves*, Oxford: Clarendon Press.
Strawson, G. 2009b. 'The Self', in B. McLaughlin (ed.) *The Oxford Handbook of Philosophy of Mind*, Oxford: Clarendon Press.
Strawson, G. 2017a. 'Mind and Being: The Primacy of Panpsychism', in G. Brüntrup and L. Jaskolla (eds.) *Panpsychism: Contemporary Perspectives*, Oxford: University Press.
Strawson, G. 2017b. 'Physicalist Panpsychism', in *Schneider and Velmans*, 374–390.
Swinburne, R. 1994. *The Christian God*, Oxford: Oxford University Press.
Swinburne, R. 1997. *The Evolution of the Soul*, rev. edition, Oxford: Clarendon Press.
Swinburne, R. 2013. *Mind, Brain and Free Will*, Oxford: Oxford University Press.
Swinburne, R. 2015. 'The Argument from Souls to God', *Religious Studies*, 51, 293–305.
Swinburne, R. 2019. *Are We Bodies or Souls?*, Oxford: Oxford University Press.
Wiggins, D. 1995. 'Substance', in A.C. Grayling (ed.) *Philosophy: A Guide Through the Subject*, Oxford: Oxford University Press, 214–249.
Williams, D.C. 1966. 'The Elements of Being', in *Principles of Empirical Realism*, Springfield, Ill.: Charles C. Thomas.
Wittgenstein, L. 1953. *Philosophical Investigations*, Oxford: Blackwell.
Wittgenstein, L. 1982. *Last Writings on the Philosophy of Psychology*, vol. I, Oxford: Blackwell.
Zahavi, D. 2011. 'The experiential self: objections and clarifications', in Siderits, Thompson and Zahavi

INDEX

abilities: experience of 31
Adams, R. 90n5
Aquinas. 72
Aristotle. 17, 82
Armstrong, D. 1n1, 47
Ayer, A.J. 33

Balaguer, M. 35
Bayne, T. 16, 23n41
Beebee, H. 89n3
Berkeley. 9, 45
beta entities 62
Black, M. 11
Blackburn, S. 91n6
Bradley, F.H. 76
Broackes, J. 17n27
Broad, C.D. 8, 14

colours 50: Colour Primitivism 51
causal closure of the physical 24
causal pairings 27
Chalmers, D. 47n4
concept empiricism 19
consensual propositions and knowledge 91
constructive empiricism 59
counterfactual conditionals: demystified 34
Craig, E. 92n10
Crane, T. 3n1
Crean, T. 71

Dainton, B. 14n22, 21n36, 86n1
Descartes. 1, 14
disseveralities 10; causal explanation of 64
Duhem, P. 22
Duns Scotus 72

embodiment 21
E=E entities 69

E+E entities 69
Empirical Atomism 19
essence and existence 69
essentially and per se ordered causal series 72
Evidential Sufficient Reason 59
Exclusion 56

Feser, E. 72–3
free decisions 31, 36; and infinite regression 37
Foster, J. 14n23, 19–20n31, 28–29
Van Fraassen, B. 59–60
Frankfurt, H. 30

Geach, P. 11n17
Ginet, C. 8n11
Goetz, S. 16–17n26
Goff, P. 46
Grunberger, R. 49n7

Hasker, W. 15n24
Heil, J. 86n1
Hong Yu Wong, 29n50
Hopkins, G. M. 5–6, 11
Hume 5, 6, 7, 19, 37, 57, 88

Identity of Indiscernibles and Dissimilarity of the Diverse 11
incompatibilism 32
Induction 62
Infinite Partition 53
introspection 6
interactionist dualism 25
Van Inwagen, P. 32
Ipseicism 46

Jackson, F. 52
Jaworski, W. 86n1

Kant 9, 14, 22
Kenny, A. 63n8
Kim, J. 25–26
knowledge 5, 92
Körner, S. 25
Kremer, E. 73
Kriegel, U. 4

Ladyman, J. 22n40
Leftow, B. 90n5
Lewis, D. 19n30, 34, 89
Lloyd, A.C. 9n13
Longuenesse, B. 9n14

McDowell, J. 51–52
McIver, A. 94
Mackie, J. 52
McTaggart, J. 2, 49–50, 54
material objects 2, 45
Maurin, A. 76–77
Miller, B. 73–78

Nathan, N. 54n17
Noonan, H. 86n1

Olson, E. 21n, 86n1

Panpsychism 46
Papineau, D. 24n43
Parfit, D. 82
Particularism 18, 76
Plato 92
primitive modality 87
Pruss, A. 57–58

qualities 3: ipseical 10, disseveral 10, unconfined 49
Quine, W. 34, 87

Robinson, H. 7n9
Ross, D. 22n40
Russell, B. 40, 52–53

Schopenhauer. 49, 54, 63
scientific realism 22
selves: definition of 1; transcendent 1, 56; ulterior 1, 40–41; unconscious 7; and death 81; and infinite mental sequences 82
Sider, T. 91n7
Simons, P. 17n27
Snowdon, P. 81n3
space 14
Spinoza 49
Sprigge, T. 85
Stein, E. 10
Strawson, G. 6n8, 21–22n37, 37–40, 46, 47–48, 86n1
Subsistent Being 69
substances 17
sufficient description 50
Swinburne, R. 7n, 11–12, 68n, 88–89, 90n

tropes 18

volition and action 9

Wiggins, D. 17n27
Williams, D C. 18
Wittgenstein, L. 63, 94

Zahavi, D. 4

Printed in the United States
by Baker & Taylor Publisher Services